THE MARRIAGE OF HAMLET

Borgo Press Drama Translations by FRANK J. MORLOCK

Alcestis, by Philippe Quinault * *Anna Karenina*, by Edmond Guiraud, from Leo Tolstoy * *Anthony*, by Alexandre Dumas * *Atys*, by Philippe Quinault * *The Boss Lady*, by Paul Féval * *The Children of Captain Grant*, by Jules Verne & Adolphe d'Ennery * *Cleopatra*, by Victorien Sardou * *Crime and Punishment*, by Frank J. Morlock, from Fyodor Dostoyevsky * *Don Quixote*, by Victorien Sardou, from Miguel de Cervantes * *The Dream of a Summer Night*, by Paul Meurice * *Falstaff*, by William Shakespeare, John Dennis, William Kendrick, & Frank J. Morlock * *The Idiot*, by Frank J. Morlock, from Fyodor Dostoyevsky * *Isis*, by Philippe Quinault * *Jesus of Nazareth*, by Paul Demasy * *The Jew of Venice*, by Ferdinand Dugué * *Joan of Arc*, by Charles Desnoyer * *The Lily of the Valley*, by Théodore Barrière & Arthur de Beauplan, from Honoré de Balzac * *Lord Byron in Venice*, by Jacques Ancelot * *Louis XIV and the Affair of the Poisons*, by Victorien Sardou * *The Man Who Saw the Devil*, by Gaston Leroux * *The Marriage of Hamlet*, by Jean Sarment * *Mathias Sandorf*, by Jules Verne & William Busnach * *Michael Strogoff*, by Jules Verne & Adolphe d'Ennery * *Les Misérables*, by Victor Hugo, Paul Meurice, & Charles Victor Hugo * *Monte Cristo, Parts One* through *Four*, by Alexandre Dumas * *The Musketeers*, by Alexandre Dumas * *The Mysteries of Paris*, by Eugène Sue & Prosper Dinaux * *Napoléon Bonaparte*, by Alexandre Dumas * *Ninety-Three*, by Victor Hugo & Paul Meurice * *Notes from the Underground*, by Frank J. Morlock, from Fyodor Dostoyevsky * *Outrageous Women: Lady MacBeth and Other French Plays*, edited by Frank J. Morlock * *Peau de Chagrin*, by Louis Judicis, from Honoré de Balzac * *The Prisoner of the Bastille*, by Alexandre Dumas * *A Raw Youth*, by Frank J. Morlock, from Fyodor Dostoyevsky * *Richard Darlington*, by Alexandre Dumas * *The San Felice*, by Maurice Drack, from Alexandre Dumas * *Saul and David Acts*, by Voltaire * *Shylock, the Merchant of Venice*, by Alfred de Vigny * *Socrates*, by Voltaire * *The Son of Porthos*, by Émile Blavet, from M. Paul Mahalin * *The Stendhal Hamlet Scenarios and Other Shakespearean Shorts from the French*, edited by Frank J. Morlock * *A Summer Night's Dream*, by Joseph-Bernard Rosier & Adolphe de Leuwen * *The Three Musketeers*, by Alexandre Dumas * *Urbain Grandier and the Devils of Loudon*, by Alexandre Dumas * *The Voyage Through the Impossible*, by Jules Verne & Adolphe d'Ennery * *War and Peace*, by J. Wladimir Bienstock & Charles Martel * *The Whites and the Blues*, by Alexandre Dumas * *William Shakespeare*, by Ferdinand Dugué

THE MARRIAGE OF HAMLET

A PLAY IN THREE ACTS

JEAN SARMENT

Translated and Edited by Frank J. Morlock

THE BORGO PRESS
MMX

THE MARRIAGE OF HAMLET

Copyright © 2010 by Frank J. Morlock

All rights reserved. No part of this book may be reproduced without the expressed written consent of the author. Professionals are warned that this material, being fully protected under the copyright laws of the United States of America, and all other countries of the Berne and Universal Copyright Convention, is subject to a royalty. All rights, including all forms of performance now existing or later invented, but not limited to professional, amateur, recording, motion picture, recitation, public reading, radio, television broadcasting, DVD, and Role Playing Games, and all rights of translation into foreign languages, are expressly reserved. Particular emphasis is placed on the question of readings, and all uses of these plays by educational institutions, permission for which must be secured in advance from the author's publisher, Wildside Press, 9710 Traville Gateway Dr. #234, Rockville, MD 20850 (phone 301-762-1305).

FIRST EDITION

Published by Wildside Press LLC

www.wildsidebooks.com

DEDICATION

My son, Miles Stanton Morlock

for his 38th birthday

CONTENTS

CAST OF CHARACTERS 9
PROLOGUE 11
ACT I 21
ACT II 89
ACT III 139
ABOUT FRANK J. MORLOCK 209

CAST OF CHARACTERS

God the Father

Abraham

Hamlet

Polonius

The Captain

Waldemar

Hans

Ophelia

Phelia (Ophelia #2)

PROLOGUE

The action unfolds in Denmark in a place in the country—seventeen years after the drama at Elsenor as told by Shakespeare.

God the Father

(In his glory) What case are we going to adjudicate today, Abraham?

Abraham

That of a dead young prince, Eternal: Hamlet of Elsenor, son of one of the last kings of Denmark. He will present himself before you accompanied by a man of ripe age and with a dead virgin in the flower of hers. They await the sentence of Divine Judgment. They've been waiting for seventeen years—

God the Father

(For whom time has no duration) Time—

Abraham

Eternal, it's measured still in terrestrial years at the gate of the Supreme Tribunal.

God the Father

You are right, Abraham—A man of ripe age, you say? And a virgin in her flower—?

Abraham

Father and daughter, Eternal, whose terrestrial names were respectively Polonius and Ophelia. Polonius was a politician of importance in the court of the kings of Denmark. He passed for wise in his plans and sagacious in his conduct. He died having received a sword blow from Hamlet through a hanging, one day when, in his capacity as a politician, he was eaves dropping—Ophelia was a wise virgin. She was said to be beautiful. As a child Hamlet loved her. It was a star crossed love. Eternal, you hadn't given to the young prince the calm soul of happy folks. Events shook him like tempests; he was uncertain like a ship on water. His formidable heredity weighed on him, like a storm which didn't explode. His destiny preceded him like a ghost, and he followed weeping over himself. Ophelia, one night, drowned herself, crazed to see the reason of her beloved prince flap in the air like the wing of a windmill—and Hamlet, assassin to avenge an assassination, died himself assassinated. Since that day,

Eternal, for the Princes of Elsenor, all was silent! A king of Norway came to rule over Denmark.

God the Father

Hamlet, Ophelia, Polonius, I'm reviewing their lives and the lives of those mingled with theirs. A benign king, an evil king, an adulterous queen—cowards and blockheads. I see rages and I see laughter, swords—masks of actors, blood and poison, hypocritical prayers and a small girl's tear, and a long series of misunderstanding dressed in garlands that men call "destiny"—Hamlet, Ophelia, Polonius we are doing an accounting of their thoughts and their intentions, Ophelia—first. What did she write in the "Book of Marble"?

Abraham

Nothing, Eternal—she never thought of opening it.

God the Father

And on the "Book of Sand"?

Abraham

The imprint of her last doll. The moral of fables that she was taught and that she didn't understand very well. The sequence of names and titles she would have borne, once married to the heir of the crown—Receipts from the kitchen. A prayer that her nurse taught some words of love she reaped from Hamlet.

God the Father

Hamlet's turn. What do you see in the "Book of Marble"?

Abraham

I see his name in big letters. Beneath it, several times he wanted to engrave "Son of the King" but the Marble was too hard or the hand too uncertain.

God the Father

And on the "Book of Sand"?

Abraham

(Reading) "I love my father, I love my mother. I love Ophelia, I love my mother less. I must avenge my father. I really love Ophelia. I love my father less since I have to avenge him. I no longer have time to love Ophelia. I wish I'd never had a father. I could love so much if "they" would leave me alone". Words, Eternal, and hearts designed in incongruous shapes. A series of hearts, pierced, crowned, embellished, beribboned. Hearts or rather a single one under several forms—

God the Father

And what about Polonius?

Abraham

In the Book of Marble—nothing. In the Book of Sand—nothing, either.

God the Father

Nothing?

Abraham

He was a politician. Ought I to make Hamlet, Ophelia and Polonius appear in your total light, Eternal Father?

God the Father

Not yet, Abraham—They've been waiting seventeen years you say?

Abraham

Yes, Eternal Father.

God the Father

What are they doing before the gate?

Abraham

They are talking of their past life.

God the Father

What are they saying?

Abraham

"If it was to do over," "If we had known what we know now." They make retrospective plans.

God the Father

What are they?

Abraham

That of forgetting who they were and of fleeing complications. To be simple. To live in isolation and quietude. They dream of a house in a clearing in a forest. "To be your wife", said Ophelia, "To prepare meals and raise our children", "No longer to mix with the great of this world nor meddle in their affairs", said Polonius. Hamlet said, "To forget that my father was King!". Evidently, they add many other things, but such is the theme of their conversation and the reason for their regrets.

God the Father

I'm thinking, Abraham.

Abraham

Your thought is infinite.

God the Father

I think that no man has lived twice, except for Lazarus who was awakened by my son Jesus.

Abraham

No man, Creator, with the exception of Lazarus.

God the Father

I think that at the Gates of Paradise where I've left them so long—they've had total leisure to reflect at length on human vicissitudes.

Abraham

What does Your Total Brilliance decide?

God the Father

(From the height of his throne) Let life be given them.

Abraham

Eternal?

God the Father

Let life be given to Hamlet, to Ophelia, to Polonius. Let them resume it at the point they left it, at the same age.

Abraham

Knowing what they know?

God the Father

Yes.

Abraham

Ah, Eternal, your wisdom is infinite! They will live like saints.

God the Father

We will see, Abraham. You will lean out golden windows. It's a spectacle I'm offering you. Awaken them from being dead. Give them the house they spoke of in a clearing in a forest. Return, them the clothes they were wearing. Give Polonius a bag of silver. Let them go.

Abraham

Creator, your mercy is infinite.

God the Father

Who knows, Abraham, if like man whom I made in my image I don't have moments of malice—me, too!

CURTAIN

ACT I

A nice little house in a clearing in a forest. In front of the house a little garden. The forest is on both sides of the house. A path passes in front of the house and disappears into the forest. From time to time, between the trees other houses can be seen. Ophelia, before the door picks roses from a climbing trellis. Polonius, spade in hand, sleeves rolled up, designs a path and pulls up weeds.

Ophelia

Father?

Polonius

My daughter?

Ophelia

I am happy—

Polonius

Me, too, I'm quite content. Let's praise God, my girl.

(They stop for a moment and eyes toward heaven, give thanks) He did for us what he didn't do for anybody. At least there's no example of it in History or Legend. For Goodness sakes, Ophelia—here we are!

Ophelia

Here we are!

Polonius

In this calm house. It's such as we wanted it to be.

Ophelia

At the entrance to a forest.

Polonius

Completely surrounded by young birch trees.

Ophelia

And there's a lake nearby.

Polonius

How easy life is going to be! Ophelia in this airy and shady garden I'm going to cultivate agreeable flowers and eatable vegetables.

Ophelia

With white roses, father.

Polonius

With roses, yes, dear girl—You will wear one on your corsage, Sundays—

Ophelia

One each Sunday—

Polonius

(Beatifically) Roses for Sundays and vegetables for every day—I'm making a path, Ophelia—The difficulty is to make it straight.

Ophelia

How pretty it will be!

Polonius

It will be pretty, but it's very difficult—Heavens, I'm going to sit down. I'm not used to this sort of work. My political tasks required lots of intelligence but less physical effort.

Ophelia

Don't think of it anymore, father.

Polonius

No, no. I'm talking to prove to myself that I no longer need to think of it. And it's so nice! Ophelia, I am a simple man who's going to marry his daughter, and getting ready to smile at his grandchildren—You are happy, my darling daughter?

Ophelia

Oh, yes, Dad! So happy!

Polonius

Here you are with your old Dad—

Ophelia

Yes—And with my Hamlet—I am indeed happy!

Polonius

You are marrying a charming young man—A bit excitable, perhaps—Events made him susceptible—but a tender heart, Ophelia—

Ophelia

Father, we're getting married in ten days—

Polonius

Yes, my girl.

Ophelia

He caused me so much pain, Dad. Oh the night I threw myself in the stream—

Polonius

Don't think about it anymore, look, my girl!

Ophelia

I can speak about it because it's all over.

Polonius

Just like me. It's nice tonight.

Ophelia

We will dine in the garden. What are you thinking about, Dad?

Polonius

Ophelia, I will have a nice end. You will close the eyes

of an old man once I've become so old that God will no longer tolerate me on earth!

Ophelia

Oh, Papa!

Polonius

In a long time. We can all wait for his clemency. My grandchildren will weep around me. Hamlet will restrain his tears, as for you, you will shut my eyes— No one had thought to do it the last time.

Ophelia

Oh, Papa!

Polonius

(Conciliatory) But we were living in a bad moment. And when this poor Hamlet ran me through—through the curtain, he was too distracted to think of rendering the last duties to me.

Ophelia

Oh! Isn't this forgotten, father?

Polonius

You are right, my girl. From talking about it, we'll end

by thinking about it—where is Hamlet?

Ophelia

He went to pick strawberries in the woods and take the air in the cool shade of trees.

Polonius

Is he actually nice to you?

Ophelia

Oh yes, Papa—Since this morning he didn't have the leisure, he ran in the woods and the surroundings. But he's as content as I am.

Polonius

And tender.

Ophelia

(Lowering her eyes) Oh, yes, Daddy.

Polonius

Dear children—(Picks up his spade) Ophelia, I've already purchased chickens from neighbor Jones and two pigs.

Ophelia

Oh, it's too much happiness, Dad.

Polonius

We've earned it, Ophelia—Have you seen the little serving girl the neighbor sent us?

Ophelia

She got here just now. She's straightening out the linen in the closets.

Polonius

Good, good. Everything is in order. (A clock strikes)

Ophelia

The Angelus.

Polonius

Let's think of God, my child—who has taken such particular care of us. Let's thank him. Let's think also of your sainted mother who left us too soon.

Ophelia

Oh—why wasn't life returned to her as well?

Polonius

(Without conviction) It's unfortunate—still—(Hamlet appears with strawberries in a little basket, flowers wrapped around his arm) Flowers in his hat.

Hamlet

Eh! Oh! Eh! Oh!

Ophelia

Hamlet! You found some strawberries?

Hamlet

Strawberries and flowers, darling. I tamed a ladybird. You see. It clings to my sleeve. Under my hat. I've brought a red and orange butterfly and a snail in my kerchief.

Polonius

What a child!

Hamlet

In my father's castle, I didn't have the leisure to interest myself in animals—Hold on! Here's the snail.

Ophelia

Oh—how small it is.

Hamlet

Yes, but what perfection! Its throat extends and retracts like that of a singer at court. We will tame it.

Ophelia

We must teach it to jump rope.

Hamlet

Polonius, give me a box of white wood. A little box which will serve as his house and we will cover it with fresh herbs.

Polonius

Hamlet, I will seek one, but I don't have one at hand.

Hamlet

A box, Polonius! A little box of white wood for the snail!

Polonius

I hear you well enough, Hamlet, but we still lack many little things. We'll find, little by little, we'll find what you need.

Hamlet

She'll run off while waiting.

Ophelia

Dad, he can't keep it in his kerchief.

Polonius

Ah, kids, how demanding you are! Tomorrow!

Hamlet

Tomorrow! One doesn't find snails everyday.

Polonius

Yes, indeed, Hamlet. (Pointing to the lawn) Hold on—here's one jumping—there—and there. You'll find a hundred for one.

Hamlet

But not like this one! Look!

Ophelia

See, Daddy—it has eyes out of its head.

Hamlet

Ah?

Polonius

Yes—

Hamlet

Ah, fine! That's fine—fine! I'll set it free—

Ophelia

Maybe we could keep it in a vase of flowers?

Hamlet

No—it's not worth the trouble, since there are others as he said. I thought it was more rare.

Ophelia

You seem to be in a bad mood, Hamlet.

Hamlet

No, no. But what's the good of snails—if only to lean over to pick them up (Raising his hat with caution) Here's the butterfly. Hold on—it's dead—I crushed it under my hat.

Ophelia

Oh—how handsome it was! Oh—the little marks on its wings.

Hamlet

Bah! This too, you must lean down to catch it. (Throws it away) It was good, it was cool.—It is fine.

Ophelia

You are happy, Hamlet?

Hamlet

Fully happy, dear fiancée. Thanks to you who are pretty, thanks to the country which is calm, and thanks to God.

Ophelia

You find me pretty?

Hamlet

The most beautiful of all.

Ophelia

(With extreme tenderness) Dear Hamlet!

Hamlet

Oh—you talk funny "Dear Hamlet"—one would think you are eating honey, you love honey? Dear Ophelia, you are pretty.

Ophelia

I please you?

Hamlet

Oh you have one eye that's smaller than the other.

Ophelia

Yes, it's true. Nurse said so.

Hamlet

Isn't it?

Ophelia

It pains me that you noticed it. Before, down there, you weren't perceptive.

Hamlet

I had troubles. Now that I have no more preoccupations, I am going to be able to look at you completely at leisure.

Ophelia

It's true, Hamlet. You no longer have anyone but me, and our dear father.

Hamlet

And your dear father—and the country.

Polonius

(Overhearing) How peaceful it is, Hamlet! What silence! Listen—only a bird-cry and the voice of an old woman bringing her animals back from the fields. We are sheltered from everything—Nothing can possibly happen. We are going to live here like snails in the pond. (Hamlet picks up a stone and hurls it toward the lake)

Ophelia

Oh—you are mean, you are going to frighten them. Why are you doing that?

Hamlet

To distract them.

Polonius

He's funny.

Ophelia

Yes, father, isn't he? Hamlet, my dear Hamlet, you will be a very amusing husband.

Hamlet

When I was ten years old, at the King, my father's court—

Ophelia

Would you please not speak of those times. We are far distant from them.

Polonius

If God gave us a second life it was so we could forget the first.

Hamlet

(In a tone of artificial apprehension) Just now, peasants passing by looked at me for a long while. I don't know if they recognized me—

Polonius

How could they recognize you—? Even if they have perceived you in the past, in their youth, they've aged since—and memory is short.

Hamlet

I don't know—something, perhaps, in demeanor and action.

Polonius

No—Don't be afraid.

Hamlet

I'm not afraid.

Polonius

Here you are a young bachelor like others. They can take you for no matter who.

Hamlet

(Without conviction) So much the better! So much the better!

Polonius

And wait, Hamlet, here come neighbors, Hans and Waldemar, to say good evening to you. You are going to see they don't take you for a Prince of Royal Blood.

Ophelia

(Insisting tenderly) Have no fear, dear hamlet. Be

completely content.

Hamlet

I am quite content. (Hans, thin, yellow and dried up appears with Waldemar—expansive cheerful, with a slack step)

Polonius

Evening, neighbors! What a charming night.

Hans

The season's been dry—we'd like to see rain fall.

Waldemar

Because, without rain—there won't be any harvest, without harvest there won't be any money, and without money there's no good beer!

Hans

Cheers to the lady—(Ophelia bows graciously)

Waldemar

And hello, comrade (Hamlet look around for the "comrade")

Polonius

Well, Hamlet—what are you looking for?

Hamlet

Ah—it's me? I was looking for the comrade. Hello, gentlemen.

Polonius

Hamlet, here are friends. My friends, I present to you my future son-in-law: Hamlet.

Hamlet

What?

Polonius

My future son-in-law. Have you already forgotten?

Hamlet

No! Oh, no. I haven't forgotten—But I was thinking of something else.

Polonius

Of what?

Hamlet

We are not here to remember.

Hans

It's plain to see you've studied with priests. You talk like an Evangelist.

Waldemar

Like a child who drank the wine Mass.

Hans

Ah, drunk-head—all you think about is drinking.

Waldemar

Yes, I love to drink. I judge the capacity of a man who can hold his drink. (To Hamlet) How many pints can you hold without bursting, comrade? When I learn your name, I'll call you by name. (Pointing to Polonius) He told me—but I forgot.

Hamlet

Hamlet—

Waldemar

Hamlet, yes. You see, your name didn't strike me.

Hamlet

Hamlet—

Waldemar

I hear you plainly—

Hamlet

It doesn't astonish you?

Waldemar

No.

Hans

It's a handsome name.

Hamlet

It doesn't remind you of anything?

Waldemar

It reminds me I had a son called Christoph, and that when he was alive, I never could recall his name,— especially as—today—he died—you see.

Hamlet

(Impatient) My name reminds you of no one?

Hans

Hold on—The son of the butcher—isn't he named Hamlet?

Hamlet

(Aggressive) Louder! Louder! To the top of the steps! Did you never hear of the son of the King—who murdered his uncle?

Polonius

(Making desperate signs) Hamlet!

Ophelia

Hamlet, dear Hamlet.

Hamlet

What? It's to show them I know History.

Hans

(Peacefully) Oh—in Denmark—we have lots of murdered kings. But, I don't know that story—I actually think our last king had no son.

Polonius

(Relaxing) Hey, hey—You see, Hamlet—There be

calm—

Hamlet

(To both neighbors) Well, gentlemen—since my name doesn't remind you of anything—so much the better! So much the better! Good evening. (A silence) (They look to him, and prepare to leave. Ophelia bustles about her household chores)

Polonius

What are they talking about in the country? What's going on?

Hans

You don't know. You've never been here—?

Polonius

No we come from a long distance.

Hans

Here we live very peacefully—

Waldemar

It's a place where one can live, drink and eat his full.

Polonius

But who governs you?

Waldemar

Nobody. Each has enough to be his own governor.

Hans

There was a Duke who raised taxes a couple of years ago. But we never see him unless he comes to hunt—

Polonius

What? Nobody lays down the law here?

Waldemar & Hans

No, Oh, no!

Polonius

Don't you find some things irritating in that situation?

Waldemar

Ah—it is bothering—yes—But it's for the best.

Polonius

(Importantly) I don't know. I don't know. There's a lot to say about it—

Waldemar

There you go. It's the best, but there'd be a lot to say about it.

Polonius

But when you don't agree about—what has happened?

Hans

They fight.

Waldemar

They drink beforehand to give themselves courage.

Hans

The rest look on.

Waldemar

They drink afterwards while telling about the battle.

Hans

The one who was beaten is obliged to give a farm animal to the winner.

Waldemar

He's the strongest who hits the hardest.

Hans

(Gently) There have to be strong and weak—that's not bad.

Waldemar

When I say the strongest I mean the one who drinks the best. That's understood.

Polonius

It seems to me you need a man of good sense to decide the rights of each.

Hans

There's the Captain.

Polonius

(Uneasily) The Captain?

Hans

When the two parties are of equal strength, we go find him to regulate the poisoned disputes; then they put two against one. (Gently) That's not bad.

Polonius

I'm thinking of a magistrate chosen by you, learned in

the statutes, a man of high erudition.

Hans & Waldemar

(Without opinion) Ah, yes—that would be nice.

Hans

Now, it's getting late.

Waldemar

Let's go eat. Good night, neighbor.

Polonius

(Persisting) We will talk about what I suggested again.

Waldemar

Glass in hand to give intelligence.

Polonius

We need to speak of it. I'm thinking only of your interest.

Hans

That's understood. If you want beautiful turkeys, come to my place. I've got the most beautiful in the land.

Polonius

Wait, my friends, I'm going to go part of the way with you—(They move away) If I lay down the law, I'll have a little platform constructed for myself under this tree. (Ophelia helped by Phelia sets the table near the climbing rose trellis)

Ophelia

Stupid, you don't know how to set a table. You place the plates, cups and glasses like a dinner for peasants.

Phelia

No, I don't know.

Ophelia

You must learn. And these long hairs in disorder—it's a suitable that you order them more decently.

Phelia

This is the way I go to Holy Mass.

Ophelia

With the village girls. If you want to follow me, you will need a suitable setting—Ah, don't cry.

Phelia

No. (And as she remains motionless, cup in hand, two tears stop at the edge of her eyes)

Ophelia

Well! Are you dreaming?

Phelia

Yes—

Ophelia

Then will you get to work! I don't dream. (The table is set. Calling.) Father—

Polonius

Here we are, darling daughter. (Entering holding Hamlet amicably by the shoulder) Yes, my dear son— Waldemar and Hans were telling me, after the Reign of Fortenbras—

Hamlet

A Norwegian, a usurper!

Polonius

What can that matter to you, Hamlet?

Hamlet

Not at all, naturally—

Polonius

Since the Reign of Fortenbras, the people have been living happily in concord and peace. Fortenbras was a great prince and his son is blessed by the people. All is well.

Hamlet

Come on, so much better! In my time, there was something rotten in the realm of Denmark. It's all been straightened out without me.

Polonius

Let's praise God, Hamlet.

Hamlet

Praise him, Polonius. But the son of Fortenbras is the son of a usurper.

Ophelia

Sit down, dear Papa. Next to me, Hamlet, like this morning.

Polonius

(Sitting softened) darling girl! Dear children! Yes, everything's going fine. But as Waldemar and Hans were telling me, the country lacks a man of sound judgment learned in the statutes. For the benefit of these good friends, since they demand it of me—perhaps, I'll agree to dispense justice.

Ophelia

Oh, yes, father. That would be an occupation for you.

Polonius

Yes, a distraction. (To Hamlet) You aren't sitting down, my dear son.

Ophelia

What are you doing, Hamlet? Are you hanging by the foot from a branch?

Hamlet

No.

Ophelia

What's the matter with you?

Hamlet

The habit of my old cloak—I lack a train of cloth.

Polonius

You are not at ease anymore.

Hamlet

I am no longer at ease. I have the impression of cutting short.

Ophelia

You will do it.

Hamlet

Yes, dear soul. (He sits down. Phelia brings a plate to the table) Summer evening. Distant shouting. An isolated song of a bird)

Ophelia

You have a young pheasant, strawberries from the forest. (Uncovering the plate) and, to begin with the fish that Hamlet caught this morning.

Hamlet

(suddenly with childish enthusiasm) My fish! It's true,

my fish. You had it roasted, Ophelia. Look at my fish. Oh—how small he is! Did it suit you well at least? Can you imagine, I had never fished? When I pulled him from the water, I had the impression of a victory. It's really a simple pleasure, isn't it?

Polonius

Yes, indeed, Hamlet. Ah, what healthy distractions we are going to have. Fishing, gardening—justice in the round open air (To Phelia who passes him a drink) Thanks, little one. (He looks at her with a wrinkled eye) Hey, hey!

Ophelia

What is it?

Polonius

This little one. Hey, hey Hamlet? Ah! You don't have an opinion. You are completely for your private meeting—your two hearts are mirrors which face each other. Dear children. (To Phelia) How old are you, little one?

Phelia

I will be seventeen on Easter, sir.

Polonius

Hey, hey! You promise, my pretty—You've got a lot already. (To Hamlet and Ophelia) Love each other, my dear children.

Ophelia

(Taking Hamlet's hand) My Hamlet!

Hamlet

(Calmly) My Ophelia. My fish has a taste of mud.

Ophelia

Lake fish always have that taste.

Hamlet

I don't know.

Ophelia

You seem annoyed.

Hamlet

No. I won't fish anymore.

Ophelia

Oh! Why? The amusing thing is to pull the fish from

the water.

Hamlet

No! To fish for fish who stink of mud, when one knows in advance they will stink of mud would be as stupid as to mount on a draught horse. One must leave them to stable-boys.

Ophelia

You will go fish in the river.

Hamlet

Oh—they'd taste of something else. No, no—I have you, Ophelia. I can give up other distractions.

Ophelia

You are happy?

Hamlet

Why, absolutely.

Ophelia

More than yesterday?

Hamlet

Yesterday, I was thoughtless in the wide open air. I was mad with happiness—But, today, I am also happy—without madness. (Phelia brings another plate)

Polonius

Ah, health and good food. Pour, my pretty. She has beautiful eyes.

Hamlet

Eyes which have looked on the sea. (To Phelia) You've lived near the sea?

Phelia

Oh, no, Milord. (She looks at him)

Hamlet

Then it's from birth.

Ophelia

Hamlet! You aren't looking at me enough.

Polonius

Hug and kiss, in love as you are!

Ophelia

Oh, father. (She kisses Hamlet who returns her kiss) Dear Hamlet! We're going to be so happy for such a long time.

Hamlet

Yes, Ophelia.

Polonius

You have a whole life in front of you! My children.

Hamlet

(Mechanically) Yes, Ophelia.

Polonius

All the time of your long youth to love each other, body and soul.

Hamlet

Polonius, you who possess such a precise mind—at what age is a man fully young?

Polonius

In character?

Hamlet

Of age! Of age! I am absolutely decided to have the character of my age.

Polonius

Until forty years of age you can count on being fully young. As for myself—at forty-two—

Hamlet

Let's not complicate it. Let's say forty. (calculating mentally) I still have nineteen years and eight months before me.

Ophelia

(Completely joyful) We've got lots of time.

Hamlet

Right, Ophelia? What a long continuation of happy days—days and days—How many days, wise Polonius?

Polonius

That's a calculation to make. (He becomes absorbed in it)

Ophelia

Hamlet.

Hamlet

Dear thing—

Ophelia

Give me your hand.

Hamlet

(Giving it to her) There—

Ophelia

We are fine—

Hamlet

Yes—

Ophelia

I would it would last forever. Alas—years pass quickly.

Hamlet

Very true. The seven thousand years that have preceded me have passed like a dream. It's the dream of today—which is long, to speak accurately, long, long, long—

Ophelia

You seem sad.

Hamlet

It's from birth.

Ophelia

Let's speak of the future to cheer you up.

Hamlet

Yes, let's talk about it! The past has one good thing about it; it's not the present.

Ophelia

Oh—what are you saying?

Hamlet

I mean when the present is already delightful, see what horizon of delights the future can open for us.

Ophelia

Where will we go?

Hamlet

Yes, where?

Ophelia

Will we live here or elsewhere?

Hamlet

The world is large—we might—

Ophelia

Oh—why not here? Father is old—he cannot travel.

Hamlet

Here, if you like—so long as he lives.

Ophelia

Oh, Hamlet—

Hamlet

I'm joking! Your dear father!

Ophelia

But sometimes we will go into the town.

Hamlet

(With real desire) Yes, yes! I really want that.

Ophelia

We will go to town to purchase what we need or like. But we won't ever go to see the actors.

Hamlet

Why?

Ophelia

Oh—I've retained the memory of a performance—before—which produced the worst effect on you.

Hamlet

Ah, at Elsenor.

Ophelia

Hush, Hamlet!

Hamlet

Ah, yes—But I brought special predispositions to it. In themselves actors are not dangerous except to themselves.

Ophelia

(Very short) No, Hamlet! No actors!

Hamlet

So be it.

Ophelia

We will flee the illuminations and the parties of the court.

Hamlet

Fine.

Ophelia

At the hour when folks crush each other to see torches and carriages, we will return prudently to hour home.

Hamlet

To our bed.

Ophelia

Oh!

Hamlet

What? In our beds if you prefer.

Ophelia

Oh!

Hamlet

Why not in "our" bed? No? Say—In our bed. In ours. You don't want to say it? Fine! Fine—It's your choice.

Ophelia

I will make you fritters; you like them, Hamlet?

Hamlet

(In a bad mood) A lot.

Ophelia

And crepes?

Hamlet

Yes.

Ophelia

You like crepes?

Hamlet

Yes—No.

Ophelia

You will love them—you will see—little by little.

Hamlet

Oh, I've plenty of time to do it.

Polonius

(Raising his nose from his notebooks) Seven thousand eighty.

Hamlet

What?

Polonius

Days. Counting each month at thirty days.

Hamlet

(Pensively) That's enormous. (A pause)

Polonius

What a nice little meal! What a charming hour of intimacy. You can clear the table my pretty—what are you looking at, Hamlet?

Hamlet

The moon above the trees.

Polonius

Yes, it's curious—and has an agreeable effect. Children, I'm going to leave you; at your age one has things to say to each other alone. Hey, hey—when you've said everything you will go to sleep.—Where's the little servant sleeping?

Phelia

In the room above the kitchen, sir.

Polonius

Come on, come on—Good night, my dear children.

Hamlet

You are going on a trip, Polonius?

Polonius

Dear Hamlet, I'm going to walk a little in the cool air of the night and greet our neighbors in passing—if I meet them. Come on, good night.

Ophelia

Good night, dear father.

Hamlet

God keeps you, Polonius. (Polonius distances himself, Phelia goes into the house)

Ophelia

How good our father is, Hamlet—there he is moving away so as not to annoy us.

Hamlet

He's right to take good habits.

Ophelia

You always joke! We really will love him, won't we? We will surround him with the tenderness of our affection.

Hamlet

We will surround him, yes, Ophelia.

Ophelia

Oh—don't you have something to tell me?

Hamlet

Yes, indeed, Ophelia, we will surround him—with—with whatever you say—

Ophelia

You are distracted, Hamlet. Hamlet—little Hamlet—my dear little Hamlet. (He looks at her) What is it?

Hamlet

Nothing.

Ophelia

Yes—you're looking at me strangely.

Hamlet

Why is it you no longer say to me "My Dear Lord" as before.

Ophelia

Yes! Didn't you hear. "My dear Hamlet!"

Hamlet

"Dear", yes. "Dear" I am well aware. But "Lord"—?

Ophelia

"Lord"—my husband?

Hamlet

My mother said "Lord" to my father even in her hours

of "effusion".

Ophelia

Yes. But your father was king—

Hamlet

I am the son of the king my father.

Ophelia

You were—in your prior life.

Hamlet

Very true! I always forget that not having titles anymore—

Ophelia

Luckily—

Hamlet

I was going to say that—I no longer have pride—no more,—Ophelia.

Ophelia

Yes?

Hamlet

You wouldn't throw yourself in the water, now, because of me?

Ophelia

In the water? Are you mad Hamlet? I was able to do it before, a day of distraction, why never, never! Don't fear anything, dear little Hamlet.

Hamlet

It's not fear—

Ophelia

You can be quite calm.

Hamlet

I am—

Ophelia

Once we are married.

Hamlet

(Interrupting her) In our bed—or in our beds?

Ophelia

Oh!

Hamlet

Say—I prefer to know in advance if you desire—or if you fear a physical understanding. If it displeases, I'll spare you, and as of now, I will remove it from my hopes and the list of my joys.

Ophelia

Oh! Hamlet! Can you say that?

Hamlet

I'm asking you—

Ophelia

(Lowering her eyes) Hamlet, you know full well that a wife belongs to her husband.

Hamlet

Then in "our"…?

Ophelia

(A breath) Yes—you desire it?

Hamlet

Oh— there's not so much joy—

Ophelia

(Tenderly) We will have it together.

Hamlet

(Suddenly coaxing) Yes, oh, yes—You are pretty—yes—(He looks at her and touches her with his fingertips. A male desire rises in him.) You have a perfect body.

Ophelia

Oh!

Hamlet

(Playing with her belt) You love me.

Ophelia

(With conviction) Yes.

Hamlet

(Troubled) Why—really? Completely? Fully?

Ophelia

Oh, yes—

Hamlet

You desire—one mystical moment.

Ophelia

(Slightly abandoned, with a sigh) Yes—

Hamlet

Ophelia—go to your room—soon I'll go to meet you—do you want it?

Ophelia

What?

Hamlet

Yes—tonight—once Polonius has gone to his room—

Ophelia

Oh—you're talking crazy—Hamlet! Oh—I shouldn't listen anymore.

Hamlet

Why?

Ophelia

Oh, Hamlet!

Hamlet

But aren't you mine? Aren't we destined for each other—for—the number of days he said?

Ophelia

Yes.

Hamlet

In that case? What does it matter whether it's ten days before or three days after?

Ophelia

(Hurt) Three nights after, Hamlet? You'd be in so little hurry?

Hamlet

I am in a hurry. I want you to be mine as of this tonight.

Ophelia

Oh no, Hamlet.

Hamlet

Why?

Ophelia

I am a virgin.

Hamlet

On the wedding night—you'll still be—

Ophelia

It's not the same thing.

Hamlet

Ah, it seems to me—Really—you don't want it tonight?

Ophelia

No indeed Hamlet—you offend me.

Hamlet

Fine—Well, you see—it seems simpler to me. And since we are condemned—I mean—since we've decided to live in complete simplicity—I thought—

Ophelia

You are crazy, Hamlet!

Hamlet

No question, I only understand simple things.

Ophelia

You don't hold it against me.

Hamlet

No, no! Your scruples make you a crown of white flowers. I really love white flowers. Perhaps, they are a little more pretentious than others—But they are white!

Ophelia

Oh—you do hold it against me—

Hamlet

No! No—no—When you threw yourself in the water, you also had a crown of flowers, right?

Ophelia

Oh, Hamlet, I don't remember—

Hamlet

I remember—roses and red flowers, right? The color of young love and young blood—You loved the red, you will love white—It's not I who reproach you for it.

Ophelia

(With dignity) Good night, Hamlet.

Hamlet

Good night, dear Ophelia—

Ophelia

You have all my heart, Hamlet.

Hamlet

We will see what's in it.

Ophelia

You are, Hamlet.

Hamlet

But in what shape?

Ophelia

Just as you are.

Hamlet

(With hope) Ah?

Ophelia

Yes, indeed—As I see you.

Hamlet

Ah, ah—Good night, dear and white fiancée.

Ophelia

(On the steps of the house) You are happy, Hamlet?

Hamlet

I think so, indeed.

Ophelia

Tell me.

Hamlet

(Pierced) I am completely happy—(She leaves, he is alone) Less than this morning—but very—very—very satisfied, I no longer have responsibilities. I no longer have a father to avenge. Then everything is fine. It was nice. The wind's a little tepid. Formerly, on the terrace of Elsenor there was also a slight breeze and coolness that came from the sea, it soothed me, like a father and slipped into my heart. I took it for a need to be loved. I was deceiving myself—it was only a sea breeze—for my first loves—which were the most fresh—will never equal its freshness—(Sings) On horseback. On my horse. I will go to greet the King of France. (stops singing) It cradled me like that when I didn't have enough experience to want to go to sleep alone.—Today, the wind comes again. But it softened on the meadow the woods, the lake, and still waters. I am really happy. I am going to lead a water-lily life. At Elsenor, in a little basin near a hovel I saw two lilies long ago—a white and yellow. A duck was turning around. Ophelia will be the white, naturally. I will be the yellow—and Polonius will be the duck. That's all.

(He sings) On horseback. On my horse.(stops singing) He said six or seven thousand eighty. Yes; oh—we won't be close to that (sings again). In a boat. In my boat. I'll go see the King of England—

What a charming night. Ophelia undressing modestly in her chamber, with nothing but moonlight, so modest is she. I am really happy—She, too. She won't throw herself in the river again. Calm has given her something of assurance in the carriage of her head and almost majestic in her demeanor. Dear Ophelia ---in short — there's a count of the days—there's no counting the nights—And they are equal in number. That's going to be marvelous. (Turns and sees Phelia —who, for a moment without budging, has been watching him) What are you doing there, little one? You haven't gone in yet?

Phelia

No, sir—

Hamlet

You are pretty.

Phhelia

Ah?

Hamlet

You don't know it. No one has thought to tell you?

Phelia

Yes, once.

Hamlet

Who?

Phelia

A lad who watched me pass on the street.

Hamlet

And then?

Phelia

He ran after me.

Hamlet

He didn't catch you?

Phelia

No—he tripped on a stone—He fell.

Hamlet

You didn't turn back?

Phelia

No, sir.

Hamlet

Maybe he really wanted you?

Phelia

If he'd really wanted me—he wouldn't have run so fast.

Hamlet

Yes—you are beautiful. There's something in you, consenting and wild—which doesn't correspond to your condition. You have the manner of the daughter of a grand chamberlain—You know that I am the son of a king?

Phelia

Ah, yes—

Hamlet

It's absolutely deprived of importance. Still, I tell you, for the situation in which you ask yourself—"Why does his head move like that, why? Why does he stride in that manner? Why's he this way and not otherwise?" I am the son of a king.

Phelia

I see plainly you do not resemble the others—

Hamlet

You've seen it?

Phelia

Yes, Lord.

Hamlet

From the first?

Phelia

Yes, Lord—

Hamlet

And yet, here, I lack a crown.

Phelia

(Respectfully) Ah? (She bows)

Hamlet

No—Oh, don't bow. I am only the ghost of a great person. I will never be king—Thank God! I'm going to live in complete obscurity. Thank God! I speak of my birth only from memory.

Phelia

Why won't you ever be king, Lord?

Hamlet

It is useless for me to tell you my story. Still, it wouldn't bore me; you must be very nice to listen to histories— and then this one of mine—I could tell it to you as if I were telling it to myself, in mixing in all that has happened to me all that is capable of happening to me—which is much more important.

Phelia

Tell me, Milord.

Hamlet

No—the best thing is for me to forget about it.—One day, perhaps—to see if I remember well—what's your name?

Phelia

Phelia

Hamlet

My goodness!

Phelia

Yes—

Hamlet

Ophelia—Phelia

Phelia

Yes—

Hamlet

You are quite pretty—you resemble Ophelia when she

wasn't so happy to live.

Phelia

I don't know.

Hamlet

She didn't know either—in those days.

Phelia

And today?

Hamlet

Her heart is full of certitudes. I don't say that enriches it. You're from the country—

Phelia

Yes, Milord—to serve you.

Hamlet

To serve me in what?

Phelia

In what you wish.

Hamlet

You know—I don't see much. Still, I will see what I can make of you.

Phelia

What you wish—

Hamlet

I'm going to get married here in a week.

Phelia

Ah?

Hamlet

Yes—a week—a week or ten days.

Phelia

It's a great happiness. (She is very sad)

Hamlet

(Not very gay) A great happiness—yes. It was indeed due me. I had so much trouble. Go to sleep little one—I'm going to sleep to.

Phelia

Have beautiful dreams, Milord.

Hamlet

Oh, no, my little girl—! I've really decided to give my imagination a rest. Let it atrophy from non-use. That's my will—I feel that Ophelia is going to help me greatly in that sense.

Phelia

Good night, Milord.

Hamlet

Good night, Phelia—go home. You are completely pretty. (Regretfully Phelia goes into the house. Hamlet remains alone for a moment. He doesn't hear Polonius come)

Polonius

Hamlet, say there, Hamlet.

Hamlet

(Without turning) Hey!

Polonius

(Jovial and promising) In ten days—

Hamlet

In ten days—yes—I am very happy, Polonius.

Polonius

What are you doing here, all alone?

Hamlet

I was watching the moon through the trees.

Polonius

For the last hour? Besides it's no longer there.

Hamlet

Exactly. I was waiting for it to return. God be with you, Polonius. (He moves away)

Polonius

Happiness doesn't make this lad intelligent.

CURTAIN

ACT II

Night. The end of a nocturnal festivity. They desert the party table in the garden. In front of the house—seated on stools or benches and even on the lawn,, neighbors—peasants—drink and snooze—some pretty girls dance and sing with young country lads—torches and lights are burning out.

Polonius

So, you are leaving us, dear and valiant Captain.

Captain

I'm going home, yes. Night's getting late. Sleep is necessary to a man at arms.

Polonius

How I understand you, dear Captain.

Captain

I have to take leave of your daughter. She's an accomplished person—modest and well behaved.

Polonius

And who will be so faithful, Captain.

Captain

She was made for a man at arms—

Polonius

(Humbly) Yes—

Captain

Your son-in-law is quite unpleasant—I am speaking to you freely—

Polonius

Ah, dear Captain he is—he's not what I would have wanted him to be—

Captain

Your daughter made a stupid marriage.

Polonius

Hamlet is a childhood friend—she really wanted to marry a childhood friend.

Captain

If she had known one. I think she would gladly have married a man—I mean a man at arms—that is to say—"A man".

Polonius

(Broken-hearted) But she'd didn't know, dear Captain. Besides, a friend from childhood—

Captain

Your son-in-law is a fool—

Polonius

He's ill. We will care for him.

Captain

God assist you—

Polonius

I hope He will.

Captain

It's a shame. Your daughter is a beautiful girl. I tell myself looking at her—very desirable.

Polonius

Why yes, desirable—me, too, I say it to myself looking at her—

Captain

I wish you good night.

Polonius

I thank you again. Ah, on the subject of this chair of justice you who are powerful and respected.

Captain

Yes, I am respected, but what can I do for you? I speak to you as a companion in arms: the marriage of your daughter is doing you the greatest harm; here you are afflicted with an idiot. Your cause is quite bad.

Polonius

Captain, dear Captain—if my son-in-law is idiotic, yes—if I'd known. I mean if she had known! Truly, this childhood friendship—was lacking—

Captain

Eh, yes! If I had married her you could have counted on this chair of justice—

Polonius

Ah—what a shame it is—! A son-in-law that I loved like a son—

Captain

I must do him justice. His stories have diverted me greatly. (Laughs stupidly) He's a jovial idiot. Ah, the night is beautiful I wish newlyweds well and consolation to the father-in-law.

Polonius

(Escorting him out) Good evening, valiant Captain. (Alone) Ah, I am desolated (Calls) Ophelia! Ophelia!

Ophelia

Father?

Polonius

I am desolated, Ophelia.

Ophelia

Why, Daddy dear?

Polonius

Consternated. Desperate. I don't know at all, my dear

girl, what annoying suggestion your fiancée—I mean your husband—obeyed.

Ophelia

Oh, father. I'm completely confused myself.

Polonius

I don't at all see what pleasure he could find in telling his story—to tell us of his childhood of the Queen, his mother, of the ghost of his father at the end of the ceremony. Are these memories to speak about, really? Was this the moment?

Ophelia

(Excusing him) Oh! Father. But he told the truth.

Polonius

(Carried away) But what's the truth? Truth that seems like a lie. I prefer a lie that seems like the truth! That is the point of departure of all good politics. With the real truth one can do nothing useful in this world! Don't reply, daughter, you don't know what you are talking about. Our friends are disposed to listen to your husband's explanations like the drivel of a man distracted. It's annoying. Now there's your Hamlet who passes for a fool once again.

Ophelia

Oh, father—

Polonius

It discredits you and me! How do you expect them to take me seriously? After this! I would have had great pleasure in doing justice under—this oak—like—I don't know who. Ah, I begin to sincerely regret having given you such a spouse!

Ophelia

Father! I am so happy to be married.

Polonius

You are happy to be married, but I would be happy to render justice!

Ophelia

Father, don't make a bad face. You know how easily offended he is.

Polonius

I know, my child, and that is not agreeable either. I endured his humor when my functions obliged me to do so. Today, as I am giving him my daughter, he might do well to make the effort to ameliorate his factious nature. Here he comes. For this time, I will say nothing to him but I am by no means satisfied. (Hamlet—appears between two neighbors leaning on the shoulder of Waldemar)

Hamlet

"To be or not to be." That's not the question at all. But to be what one is, you understand?

Waldemar

No. (They pass)

Ophelia

(To Polonius) Father, isn't it time I withdraw into my chamber?

Polonius

Ah, always like your sainted mother. She, too, on the night of our wedding manifested a quite similar impatience which was not given the lie by what followed. Yes! If you wish! No, wait. Ah! You see I am so desolated that I don't know what I ought to do. Go see if the serving girl has cleared the table and extinguished the torches—

Ophelia

Yes, father. (Passing near Hamlet) Hamlet.

Hamlet

Hey?

Ophelia

(Low) Till soon, Hamlet.

Hamlet

Certainly, my dear Ophelia.

Ophelia

(Lower still) I'm going to go to my room.

Hamlet

Fine. Perfect. Till soon. (He returns to his conversation, Ophelia leaves) You understand, dear Waldemar. The two of you must understand what I said—that I cannot find great pleasure in fishing for frogs and that playing with bowling balls cannot interest me.

Hans

That's understandable.

Waldemar

I actually understand that fishing has no attraction for a man who has been resuscitated from the dead. (They elbow him jovially)

Hamlet

(Completely preoccupied) Dear friends. I had hoped in a second life to distract myself a little more than in the first. But I've nothing to do; I don't find any distraction corresponding to my nature, to my condition, to my birth. You understand? You understand?

Waldemar

In short, what you need is another ghost. Isn't that right, Hans?

Hans

(Low) Shut up, will you.

Waldemar

I'm shutting up. (To Hamlet) Good night, Lord—Prince Hamlet—

Hamlet

Good night, my friends! Good evening.

Hans

(Pulling Waldemar) Come, my drunkard. Now there's a table cloth already—go find your dog's chain and don't waste time. We are going to laugh. (They move off—Hamlet and Polonius remain alone)

Hamlet

Well, Polonius?

Polonius

My son?

Hamlet

You seem depressed, Polonius? It's nice weather, isn't it?

Polonius

Yes—

Hamlet

The night is cool.

Polonius

Yes—

Hamlet

It's not cold.

Polonius

No.

Hamlet

I find it a beautiful night.

Polonius

Very beautiful.

Hamlet

Despite its coolness.

Polonius

Yes, despite that.

Hamlet

Or because of its coolness.

Polonius

Or because of its coolness—

Hamlet

(Exasperated) Ah—

Polonius

What?

Hamlet

I wanted to hear you say something.

Polonius

What? What do you want me to say?

Hamlet

"Words! Words! Words!"

Polonius

Ah, words! I scorn words. And you ought to follow my example. I know too well where words have led you!

Hamlet

Yes. Oh, yes—I understand you, wise Polonius. But, all the same, from time to time, a good little word with a double meaning—with an equivocation—which allows a trail like a splinter in the flesh. I said, "This evening is beautiful", and you replied "It's beautiful". From time to time, I'd like a "Who knows?" a "We shall see what it will be tomorrow" a "God alone is God" some clever reply signifying doubt, on which my thought can employ itself—For exercise—As one does with armies. (And as Polonius reacts with great impatience—discouraged) Hey? You aren't leaving, Polonius!

Polonius

Hamlet—you make me despair. I prefer to withdraw—because I have too many things to tell you. Still, I build some hope on the night you are going to spend—but I don't approve of your shameless wit. I don't approve at all. Till tomorrow, Hamlet.

Ophelia

(Emerging from the house, after a moment circling around Hamlet) Hamlet.

Hamlet

Dear thing.

Ophelia

I'm going to go in, Hamlet—

Hamlet

(Says nothing)

Ophelia

(Modest and coaxing) In "our" room.

Hamlet

(Politely) You're tired?

Ophelia

I might be, Hamlet. A day like this!

Hamlet

Very tiring! To whom do you speak? Very tiring!

Ophelia

(Eyes lowered, trying to put her head on Hamlet's breast) But I am not.

Hamlet

How did you picture your wedding, Ophelia, if you happened to think of it, in the past?

Ophelia

(Excitedly) As it passed, dear Hamlet.

Hamlet

Right. You have no imagination.

Ophelia

And what about you?

Hamlet

Me, personally? (Dreaming for a moment) I saw a small girl on a horse too large for her. I saw myself on a horse too big for me. We galloped through the trees—and the stars, naturally.—She went before me lost in fear, but her fear was willing. Suddenly, I caught up with her, I took her in my arms, and I placed her on my saddle, folded over like a caught bird. We began the race on two horses. We continued the race on one—on mine!

Thus the wedding ceremony appeared to me in its delirium, its enchantment and its consequences. It was a sort of dream.

Ophelia

You are still barely awake, Hamlet. Shake yourself.

Hamlet

Soon I will go join you, dear thing, and that will wake me up completely.

Ophelia

You seem sad, Hamlet.

Hamlet

(With an internal fever) Me? Ah, if you knew how full

of passion I am.

Ophelia

(Troubled) Oh, Hamlet—Hush!

Hamlet

(In sweet scorn) Yes, oh, yes! I hear you, dear pigeon. No—an ardor which feels cramped. I had thought that I would consent to live gently attached to it—like a sheep browsing in a field. Alas, that sheep doesn't like grass.

Ophelia

I don't understand you, Hamlet! What sheep? (Very tenderly—promising all) Come, Hamlet!

Hamlet

Where?

Ophelia

Come—

Hamlet

Ah, yes—I was speaking to you of sheep, you think of the ram—that one,-- I don't know very well what it's worth. Go, Ophelia: he's going to join you. (And as she doesn't understand) I'm going to join you.

Ophelia

You said "the ram"?

Hamlet

Yes, my innocent. Go—my white flower—I'm coming, my little lamb.

Ophelia

Should I light the lamp, Hamlet?

Hamlet

It's not worth the trouble, my heart. God needs no light to see us. (She moves away, going into the house and closing the door behind her) I've never been happy. Well, happiness is still the saddest thing in the world.

(Hans appears disguised as a ghost, wrapped head to foot in a white veil. Waldemar follows him on tip-toe and hides in the shadow. The ghost takes a position and gestures. Soon Waldemar behinds a tree rattles chains and imitates the cry of a hoot-owl)

Ghost

Hamlet.

Hamlet

Oh—a ghost!

Ghost

(Louder) Hamlet.

Hamlet

(Delighted) A ghost.

Ghost

(Still louder) Hamlet.

Hamlet

I'm listening—if you knew how I'm listening.

Ghost

Hamlet! I'm the ghost of your grandfather.

Hamlet

Oh. "Dear old geezer," what do you say?

Ghost

I am the ghost of your grandfather, very tall, very powerful and venerated king of Denmark, Tristan the Sad—that his son, young rogue of a father, caused to die with needle punctures.

Hamlet

Interesting! Do tell! But, how was he able to murder you, since you died in your bed?

Ghost

One evening, at a banquet, your father amused himself by pricking me with a needle, in the back, to distract me, he said. And I laughed indeed, like a fool, seeing my great age. But your father had dipped his needles in a mortal poison whose action is unsuspected—and I died three weeks later.

Hamlet

Horrible, horrible, horrible! My venerated father was a murderer.

Ghost

Your father had accomplices. These accomplices had sons. One is today a great Marshall, another is a cook in the court of Fortenbras—Hamlet, my death has not been avenged!

Hamlet

(Enthusiastically) I knew indeed that there must remain something rotten in the court of Denmark.

Ghost

Hamlet, I demand vengeance!

Hamlet

Sainted grandfather, this is my concern. I knew indeed thesre remained wish for me.

Ghost

Goodbye, Hamlet.

Hamlet

Good bye, good ghost: sleep in peace—this is my affair! I thank you once again. I was unable to accustom myself to a life without responsibility. It's vain to be the son of a murdered king; one is nonetheless the son of a king. Thanks, grandpa! We are going to release the sheep. (Laughter can be heard. Waldemar helps Hans get out of the white veil. They watch Hamlet with shining eyes running back and forth)

Hamlet

A horse! A horse! Elsenor is in the North! (Arms crossed he heads the North) Here's the North! A sword!—Ah, here's that of the Captain. A horse! I won't find one this evening. Good! I'll leave tomorrow. Besides, a wedding night is not to be disdained. Tomorrow! Yes, yes, tomorrow! (Falls on his knees) Ah, My God!

Thanks, My God! You've resuscitated me—and now you give me life. Give me also the courage to fulfill my own destiny. (Polonius appears in the doorway)

Polonius

Hamlet—I really don't know how to advise you to show your wife a bit more urgency. It's a day in which it is "de rigueur"—That's the word: "de rigueur"—Allow me to tell you....

Hamlet

Polonius, I am saying my prayers—

Polonius

You ought to say them together, Hamlet.

Hamlet

That's not possible, Polonius. Not everyone speaks to God in the same tone.

Polonius

As you like, but imagine that this young girl is waiting feverishly in the wedding room—I said the word "feverishly".

Hamlet

You must go calm her down, Polonius. Tell her to stay at the window while waiting. (Polonius shrugs his shoulders and goes back in the house. Hamlet keeps his prayerful attitude) Lord, I really want to get out of here. (Rises and sees Phelia standing quietly a few steps from him) Heavens, there you are Phelia, what are you doing here?

Phelia

I am watching you, sir.

Hamlet

Ah, how do you like me?

Phelia

You are handsome.

Hamlet

It's possible. What are you thinking about?

Phelia

She's going to be happy.

Hamlet

Who?

Ophelia

She—

Hamlet

Ah, Ophelia?—Why?

Phelia

(With a little gesture) You are going to go to her.

Hamlet

You seem to regret it. (She makes a small gesture with her shoulders) What's wrong with you? Why are you turning your head away? Why? Heavens! A tear. Why, are you crying?

Phelia

(Sobbing) I'm not crying.

Hamlet

I have the impression that if I took you in my arms you wouldn't protect yourself. (He pulls her to him)

Phelia

I love you.

Hamlet

You are very beautiful. Oh—how cool your lips are. (Curiously) You love me?

Phelia

Yes.

Hamlet

My goodness!

Phelia

I'd really like to die.

Hamlet

In short, I can do with you what I will—if I will?

Phelia

Yes.

Hamlet

You are really sweet—But what!

Phelia

Yes, you love her—

Hamlet

No.

Phelia

I thought so.

Hamlet

Me, too.

Phelia

You loved her yesterday.

Hamlet

I was waiting for the next day.

Phelia

This morning, leading the procession, the length of the fields—you were singing and you were following the humming birds with the eyes of a man content.

Hamlet

This morning—yes.

Phelia

You entered the church with such a firm step.

Hamlet

I was going towards a miracle. I always count on seeing one when I go to church.

Phelia

And here it is the evening of the wedding—

Hamlet

Yes—

Phelia

She seems very happy.

Hamlet

Who? Ophelia? Yes—But she seems too much to believe that this happiness is owed her.

Phelia

You don't love anyone?

Hamlet

If I must love someone, maybe I'll love you. But to

love—

Phelia

You no longer want to—?

Hamlet

Bah—As soon as "they" know you love them "they" forget you are the son of a king.

Phelia

Oh—Milord.

Hamlet

Yes—they say that before. But very quickly they employ diminutives and whisper to you with the names of animals.

Phelia

Milord, milord!

Hamlet

So on a day of weakness if I come to weep on your shoulder—there, at the nape your neck—you will see if you still call me "Milord". (Takes a step)

Phelia

(Pale) You are going to her?

Hamlet

Yes—it's late.

Phelia

Goodbye, Lord.

Hamlet

Why "goodbye"? Till tomorrow.

Phelia

No—

Hamlet

You won't be here any longer?

Phelia

No—

Hamlet

You intend to leave?

Phelia

Yes—

Hamlet

You are jealous?

Phelia

I am not jealous. I'm in pain.

Hamlet

Heavens! Usually "they" are comfortably jealous and never know how to have pain. You are truly exceptional! And you cry without drying your eyes! Generally, they dry their eyes without crying.—Where do you intend to go?

Phelia

I don't know.

Hamlet

To the town.

Phelia

Oh—no.

Hamlet

Where? (She says nothing. At each question her shoulders throb) Far from here? No? You have too much pain, you say? You are thinking of dying? You aren't thinking of the lake?

Phelia

(In her tears) Oh! No.

Hamlet

No? Speak up? You aren't thinking of that? Yes, yes—you are thinking of that! (Her face immediately clears up) You would do that? Her big eyes all soaked—There's the place you want to go.

Phelia

I loved you—

Hamlet

Come on! Don't have any more pain. Don't be jealous. I won't go! I'm not going there. Heavens. I will leave her to her satisfied virginity.

Phelia

Truly?

Hamlet

Yes.

Phelia

You are married?

Hamlet

In my capacity as son of a King, I don't experience annoyance in repudiating my wife. In every way, I would have left her, I must leave tomorrow; I'm going to leave tonight. The night is cool—do you know who, in the area, could lend me a horse?

Phelia

(Altered) You are going to leave?

Hamlet

Yes—

Phelia

Where are you going?

Hamlet

To Elsenor, to avenge grandpa, overthrow the reigning king, or—If I reach an understanding with him, to take command of the army or navy and leave to carve out a kingdom of my own. Sweetness is not worth much to me, and I understand nothing of happiness. Why are you looking at me like this? Your eyes are that of a child who's going to ask for a very expensive toy.

Phelia

I want to follow you.

Hamlet

I don't need anyone.

Phelia

I won't bother you.

Hamlet

You would ask me where I am going.

Phelia

I would wait until you told me. Take me with you.

Hamlet

You would be a pretty thing to take along. But as we went, you would lay down your conditions.

Phelia

No—since you are my lord.

Hamlet

You recognize it?

Phelia

Yes, indeed—

Hamlet

Well—but! No, I cannot take you. I am not certain of finding a horse for myself—how would I be able to find one for you?

Phelia

You could take me on yours.

Hamlet

(Struck) On mine? Heavens! On mine! Truly? You want that?

Phelia

At least, I would be sure of following you everywhere. You really want it? You really want it.?

Hamlet

Perhaps.

Phelia

I love you so much!

Hamlet

You want to be the companion of a hero!

Phelia

Oh, yes.

Hamlet

Listen to me, Phelia. I didn't say a "heroine" but "the companion of a hero"—as might be said of the victim of his inclination.

Phelia

(Looking at him) Oh, yes.

Hamlet

You understand me plainly?

Phelia

No. But, perhaps, little by little, you will explain to me.

Hamlet

(Delighted) Oh, dear love! You don't understand me, and you admit it?

Phelia

Yes.

Hamlet

Come! I'll take you! You will be a true companion! It's when they assure you they understand you that they know nothing at all. We are going to live very happy.

Phelia

(Trembling a little) You think so?

Hamlet

Very much! Yes—I don't know exactly what I could give you of me. But I hope you won't be bored. (She looks at him, happy and sad) No, you won't be bored. You will have trips, unforeseen ones. And then you will console me, you will look at me—you will study the changes and the variations of my moods.

Phelia

(Hesitating) You'll be concerned about me—sometimes—a little bit?

Hamlet

Naturally: I will tell you my memories of childhood, and my pains from all times—We are going to be happy. I love glory and I don't fear death.

Phelia

Oh—we are going to die.

Hamlet

Naturally.

Phelia

Together?

Hamlet

Separately. Unless an accident unforeseen—independent of my will—you have beautiful eyes. Come!

Phelia

Yes. (She looks at him fearfully, ready to recoil)

Hamlet

What's wrong with you—?

Phelia

I'm coming.

Hamlet

One would say you are afraid.

Phelia

Oh, no.

Hamlet

Yes, you're afraid.

Phelia

A little.

Hamlet

Of death.

Phelia

No.

Hamlet

Of the life I'm offering you. In that case, Phelia, if the heart in you says—if you are already Ophelia , stay with Ophelia ; she will make you crepes on Sundays and fritter during 7080 days.

Phelia

No. I don't want that!

Hamlet

In that case, come, Phelia. Let's leave!

Phelia

Yes. (He takes her arm) Where are we going?

Hamlet

Already!

Phelia

No, no—it's not a question! I was saying that—

Hamlet

Don't ask for precision, Ohelia. What's it to you where I am going, since truly, we won't go to the end together.

Phelia

You will abandon me?

Hamlet

Don't anticipate! Don't anticipate!

Phelia

I would like to know—

Hamlet

She wants to know, and she is so pretty when she says "I don't know". Don't shed your blossoms before your time. Live a little in your ignorance.

Phelia

As you wish, you are the master.

Hamlet

Fine! One cannot say enough about these things. Do you want to give me your lips—?

Phelia

Yes—(Her eyes are full of tears. He kisses her)

Hamlet

Are you satisfied?

Phelia

I have some pain, but I am satisfied? I would have wanted—

Hamlet

Hush let's go. (He pulls her)

Polonius

(Emerging from the house) Well, Hamlet.

Hamlet

My goodness! Polonius. Good evening.

Polonius

I assure you Hamlet that your wife is losing patience.

Hamlet

Her virginity weighs on you? Polonius you are a demanding father. Good night, dear father—take my wishes to Ophelia.

Polonius

Where are you going?

Hamlet

I'm following the route. When I am at its end I will turn right or left.

Polonius

Right or left? This evening? You mock my white hair, Hamlet!

Hamlet

I'm not mocking, Polonius and your hair is fine where it is. Ah, you who know the country-folk here, point someone out to me who can loan me his horse—He will be rewarded a hundred times like the garden of the King of Kings.

Polonius

A horse? You need a horse?

Hamlet

To travel, Polonius. To go more quickly.

Polonius

But where are you going?

Hamlet

To the court of Fortenbras. I desire to shed light on several obscure stories, to extract vengeance if need be, to recover my wealth and my titles, all --at least the attributes of my birth right. Good night.

Polonius

Hamlet—be reasonable! My dear Hamlet, go inside your home.

Hamlet

I am full of reasons, Polonius. I demand a horse from you to go home.

Polonius

What do you lack here?

Hamlet

A royal mantle and a crown.

Polonius

You have Ophelia.

Hamlet

I'm demanding a crown, not a chain—Good evening!

Polonius

Hamlet, it's not possible! (Calling) Ophelia! Ophelia! Hamlet—you've had too much to drink. You've been drinking all day on your wedding! Hamlet, listen to me. (Ophelia appears) Daughter, keep him here. Go take him by the hand. Drag him into your little room. Forget the conventions for once. Go my daughter, his poor head is wandering. (Ophelia goes to take Hamlet by the arm, Polonius leaps—clapping his hands before them) Well, Hamlet! Now here's a handsome little couple. Huh, Hamlet? The loosened hair—these shoulders—Huh? Lucky lad! I'd like to be in your place.

Hamlet

Polonius, don't play the go-between siren. You are not seducing me. Ophelia, I'm going to live, I have important business. Sleep well tonight and for 7080 days, seek somebody other than me. Come Phelia (To Phelia)

Ophelia

Father he's taking Phelia with him. Oh! Oh!

Polonius

This isn't true, Hamlet? A chamber—maid. You couldn't give me such an affront.

Hamlet

Polonius, let's not prolong our goodbyes.

Polonius

My daughter, he's leaving you, he's leaving his wife.

Ophelia

Hamlet!

Hamlet

What?

Ophelia

Don't leave! I love you! My dear husband, I am your wife.

Hamlet

No question—sons of Kings must have daughters of Queens—

Ophelia

What's going to become of me?

Polonius

What's going to become of me? Ah, if only she were a

widow.

Hamlet

You will dissolve the marriage in Rome.

Polonius

Who would want her now—with such a small dowry?

Hamlet

Hold on Polonius. Here's my necklace. They put it around my neck the day I was ten years old. The medallion contains hair from my incestuous mother. The hair has no value but you can sell the jewel for a 1000 florins. That's a dowry. (Tosses the necklace to Polonius) To all a good night! (To Phelia) Come Phelia.

Ophelia

(Completely distracted) Hamlet—My dear father.

Polonius

Hamlet.

Hamlet

Go back to your rooms.

Polonius

(Maddened, turning on himself) My God! Somebody! Somebody! Prevent him from leaving! I know what this is. It's a crisis of retrospective despair. He needs to stretch out in his bed. In his bed—and some chicken soup.

Hamlet

Polonius, Polonius, you are talking like a fish seller.

Polonius

Hamlet! For the last time.

Hamlet

Polonius, I'm not going to listen to you anymore; even if I wanted to I couldn't do it. Something is between us.

Polonius

What?

Hamlet

A tapestry. Good evening, my master.

Polonius

Don't let him leave. I'm opposed to it. I'm opposed to it.

Hamlet

What? What's wrong with him? A rat? It's a rat? A fat rat, perhaps? Ah, ah, Polonius we know the fate of fat rats. (Pulls his sword)

Polonius

Help. A mad man! All is lost. I'm withdrawing. I've lived too much. Once too much.

Hamlet

Twice too much!

Polonius

(Dragging Ophelia away) Come, Ophelia. He is dead for us—and we won't wear mourning for him!

Hamlet

I am wearing it for myself. (They go in the house and lock the door) Come, Phelia—Heavens, she's asleep. She's not prepared for strong emotions. Poor little thing. (Calling her gently) Phelia! Phelia! Phelia! She's really sleeping. She's perhaps dreaming that her good will proves to be the strongest, that our love is more robust than I believe, and that it will live like an old oak. It's in the dream that is no longer understood.

If I had met her when I was fourteen, I would not have done her ill. I would have wept at her throat, I would have slept on her shoulder—exactly as she is sleeping on mine—dreaming. She's really sleeping. (Calls her low)

Phelia, Phelia—Hamlet are you going to do ill this little thing who's sleeping as you never knew how to sleep? Don't be cruel with her. You will have so many occasions to be with yourself. Phelia, I wish you fine nights. You've procured me three or four agreeable ones. But what? I am not capable of being nasty in the moon light. That's a deficiency in my education. I feel like crying as if I were unhappy. (Looking at Ophelia who sighs in her sleep, then pulling a ring from his finger) I intended this ring for the first woman who would understand me. She understood me in this sense—that she accepted me without quibbling.

Then she said to me, "you are the master". She understood me as much as possible. Naturally, it didn't last. Still, she had the good taste to doze off before expressing any of those irreparable stupidities that they all suck in with milk. I am giving you my ring, Phelia. You are pretty, you are very pretty. You benefit from every view-point by being seen in moonlight. (Knee on the ground, he places the ring on her finger)

Dame Phelia, Princess of Elsenor, Queen of Denmark. There—let's speak of it no more.

(Rising, dusting off his knee, adjusting off his trousers) Ophelia, Phelia—Ophelia, Phelia.

Hamlet

My goodness! I've got two wives. I've joined them already in my head. I have not sinned. My God. I am going to confuse them very quickly, and the day of forgetfulness come. I will only have to renounce them once. Goodbye little ones. (Moving away, singing in a clear voice)

A horse

On my horse

I will go greet the King of France

CURTAIN

ACT III

Autumn: The dinner hour. A bell rings.

Polonius

Dear Captain, I've seen the Archbishop. Be happy as much as this beautiful girl is herself. Her deplorable marriage will be dissolved in a very short time. My dear children all that remains for me to do is to bless your marriage.

Captain

Ah, I am very lucky. She's a beautiful girl.

Ophelia

Oh, Captain

Captain

Made for a man of arms—I always said so.

Polonius

We always thought so. (With nonchalant melancholy) She was the enchantment of my old age. She will make your age ripe.

Ophelia

Father, don't be sad.

Polonius

No, child, I don't have the leisure—besides, my new duties are going to absorb me greatly.

Captain

When will you render justice for the first time?

Polonius

As soon as possible; there's such a need for justice.

Captain

Let me know in advance; I will be there, and if you need assistance do call on my arm. It's been a long while since I made war; and I need to exert myself if only for my health.

Polonius

(To Ophelia) You will have a good, intelligent husband, my dear girl—and handsome.

Captain

Solid, I can say that. And that's not displeasing to women—And yet! It's at night we're worth our price, the rest of us.

Polonius

Eh, eh—!

Ophelia

(Blushing artfully) Oh, Captain!

Polonius

Hug me, kids! I am really happy about this marriage. (He hugs them)

Captain

(Taking his leave) Au-revoir, dear beauty. (He leaves)

Polonius

He's indeed a good-looking man—

Ophelia

Oh, yes, father.

Polonius

Look-you, dear daughter. Here at this level of low branches I'm going to put the judge's bench—above it, on a bench, my chair and for you, daughter, and for our Captain. I'll have them place two stools—on the lower steps—one on each side.

Ophelia

And who are you going to judge?

Polonius

I don't know yet, dear girl. I would really like to find a guilty person; but with the help of God—we will. Ah, here's our Ophelia coming to wash your white collars.

Ophelia

I've already asked you father, not to give her the name of Ophelia—it resembles mine too much.

Polonius

You are right. Well, Gertrude—handsome linen! Beautiful white collars! Hey, hey—beautiful little girl—hey, hey—

Ophelia

Father.

Polonius

We don't have lovers in the country, hey! We won't find her in love. I know it, I know it. (Phelia moves away without replying)

Polonius

She has a pretty sly look—not displeasing, this little one—very—

Ophelia

(Outraged) Father, I no longer want you to pay attention as you've been doing to this wench, this scullery maid.

Polonius

No, my daughter. It was a joke. Do you imagine that I am a man who doesn't respect himself, come on. And the memory of your sainted mother—come on.

Ophelia

You drink too much, Daddy.

Polonius

My Ophelia, I repeat to you every day—I won't drink anymore.

Ophelia

And you ought to have kicked this serving girl out.

Polonius

Indulgence, you know.

Ophelia

A ruined girl.

Polonius

Dear child, it's this Hamlet who turned her hand.

Ophelia

(Stamping her feet) Ah—that one—may he never return.

Polonius

Don't worry—dear girl, he died in prison.

Ophelia

Let him leave us in peace!

Polonius

Yes, Ophelia. Let him leave us alone. Everything's going fine. I'm going to render justice—and the Captain is a handsome man.

Ophelia

Suppose he came back?

Polonius

I will kick him out!

Ophelia

Yes, father—right.

Polonius

Like a dog, Ophelia, I swear it.

Ophelia

Without hesitating, father!

Polonius

Do you take me for a man who doesn't know what he wants? Like a dog—with kicks and blows with a pitchfork.

Hamlet

(In the distance, leaning on the trunk of a large tree) Hello, Ophelia, hello, Polonius.

Ophelia

Oh, father.

Polonius

Everything was going so well.

Ophelia

Kick him out, father—

Polonius

Yes, yes—leave it to me.

Ophelia

I'm going to find a pitchfork.

Polonius

No, wait—wait. He has rights over you, let's not forget it. The marriage has not yet been annulled and perhaps he's in good at court. (Prudently, advancing a step) Hello, Hamlet. You are quite dusty.

Hamlet

The roads are dusty.

Polonius

Your health is good. (Hamlet remains silent) Why didn't you come back on horseback?

Hamlet

To return less quickly.

Polonius

(Suspicious) You saw the King, Hamlet?

Hamlet

I saw him—

Polonius

You didn't overthrow him?

Hamlet

No, Polonius.

Polonius

Thank God, our Lord and Master, for our good and all is still on his throne, in good health and living well—

Hamlet

Yes, living well, Polonius—as they say.

Polonius

He deigned to listen to you, with benevolence?

Hamlet

He didn't listen to me; I had nothing to tell him.

Polonius

You did the right thing—And what did our King have to say to you?

Hamlet

Nothing, Polonius.

Polonius

Still, he gave you an audience?

Hamlet

I didn't ask one of him.

Polonius

Are you mad, Hamlet?

Hamlet

Just tired, Polonius.

Polonius

You just told me that you had seen the King.

Hamlet

I did see him, one morning, emerging from Elsenor on horseback. His trumpets woke me up. I'd been sleeping at the foot of a tree. He passed by, I was seated near the tree.

Polonius

(Speechless) Seated near the tree?

Hamlet

Thanks again—he looked nice.

Polonius

At the foot of a tree.

Hamlet

He seemed well fed to me.

Polonius

I don't understand.

Hamlet

I was on foot. The King on horse. What's astonishing about a King of Denmark being on horseback?

Polonius

Why didn't you speak to him?

Hamlet

To the horse?

Polonius

I beg you, Hamlet—to the King!

Hamlet

Because, around that time I realized I had nothing to tell him.

Polonius

And your thirst for vengeance?

Hamlet

Around that time I realized I had no one to avenge.

Polonius

Ah unconsciously. To have poisoned our life and our happiness in our first life by a legitimate need for vengeance—although exaggerated! Exaggerated!

Hamlet

Yes, I ask you for forgiveness, Polonius.

Polonius

To have led Ophelia to despair and death—as if by hand. (He taps his hand) Dear child—poor blameless heart and Laertes my irreproachable son—and your late mother—and myself—we still have mockeries, humiliations—misunderstandings—in a second life given to us—let's be blunt about it-- by the excessive kindness of the Creator. To have done all that!—To come one day to coldly declare that it was perfectly useless, and that, all things considered, you have no one to avenge! I thought that at all times, Hamlet, but it is painful for me to hear you say it.

Hamlet

Polonius, The Kings of Denmark are dead of a death which clamors for vengeance. This one killed that one. Where did the crime begin? Who was the first criminal? It would be good to know—but those are histories of Kings. I have nothing kingly in my family.

Polonius

He is mad! Dear daughter, here is Hamlet returned, but sicker than ever. He no longer knows what he's talking about.

Hamlet

Yes, Polonius. I'm saying that I no longer have a role in the histories of Kings. Did you know the Reverend Father Oswald who used to be the confessor of the, Queen, my mother?

Polonius

And mine; he baptized Ophelia.

Hamlet

He's very old and very garrulous. And in his need to tell stories relating to great persons, he mixes in a few secrets from the Confessional—with his personal memories.

Polonius

I don't understand.

Hamlet

Thanks to him, the common depths of court scandals is enriched bit by bit. Intact reputations are destroyed.

Some virtuous reputations have gone with the flow. Closed boxes are opened—the mystery of my birth was contained in one of them. It emerged from its box and it was passed from hand when I arrived in Elsenor —I learned it in an inn where I was making my first change of horses.

Polonius

A mystery?

Hamlet

Yes, Polonius.

Polonius

And what was so extra ordinary about your birth?

Hamlet

Extraordinary? Let's not exaggerate—like many others I am not the son of my father.

Polonius

(Speechless) Whose son are you then?

Hamlet

The son of another father—a legitimate father.

Polonius

Could you be the son of the King—Your uncle—who you murdered?

Hamlet

Don't complicate, matters, Polonius. I told you, I am not of royal blood.

Polonius

Ah, ah, the Queen had a weakness for one of her gentlemen—? Who is your father?

Hamlet

Thomas Woolworth.

Polonius

What?

Hamlet

Thomas Woolworth

Polonius

I didn't know him.

Hamlet

You didn't know Thomas Woolworth? You didn't know my father?

Polonius

Who was he?

Hamlet

A stable boy.

Polonius

What?

Hamlet

Yes, Polonius.

Polonius

(Voice, trembling with hope) Are you quite sure of what you are saying?

Hamlet

My real father kept horses and lived in the stable, yes. So then, Polonius, you who served the one I called "my uncle" to the detriment of the one I called "my father"—that you betrayed—to this one—or that one—or both—I no longer have to concern myself about it, I don't have to take their cause in hand and I don't think you ever did the least harm to my father the stable boy—he was a very obscure man. I will admit to you that I didn't have the heart to find out where my father's tomb is or of what death he died. I've been filial like that enough.

(A change is visible in the attitude of Ophelia and Polonius. Ophelia rises, head back, nostrils narrowed. Polonius snickers, arms folded, taking a breath, chest bulging)

Polonius

Ah, my lad—! I knew you insolent! It was the odor of hay which mounted to my nose, then?

Hamlet

Don't be harsh, Polonius. You know that I won't reply to you—I feel I no longer have the right to hoist a royal soul—nor the desire—I've lowered my tent.

Polonius

Get out. You have no more business here.

Hamlet

In what way is my sight hurtful to you, Polonius?

Polonius

Get out of here mountebank I've always detested you, anyway son of son of…

Hamlet

Son of a stable boy, Polonius.

Polonius

Get out of here! I was capable of giving you my daughter—Do you intend to leave?

Hamlet

Where do you want me to go, Polonius? I need to eat and sleep. Give me asylum.

Polonius

You are not proud.

Hamlet

My father must not have been much. Why should I be more than my father?

Polonius

Ah, ah—you hear, Ophelia? (To Hamlet) So you intend to spend the night here?

Hamlet

The night, Polonius—and all day tomorrow and others. I don't know anyone in the world.

Polonius

(Smiling over some base idea) So be it. I really want to let you live here.

Ophelia

Oh, no, father.

Polonius

Wait! You are going to see. (To Hamlet) On condition that you work to earn the bread I give you.

Hamlet

That's quite natural, Polonius.

Polonius

I will entrust you with the only work that you are capable of.

Hamlet

What's that?

Polonius

You will keep my pigs. (A smile of gratitude from Ophelia)

Hamlet

That seems to me to be appropriate, Polonius, given my base birth.

Polonius

Henceforth, you'll have to respect me like your lord, you understand? There's no more "Polonius".

Hamlet

(Agreeably) Perhaps there never was one.

Polonius

(Majestically) As your lord, you understand. Ah, ah—that's going to hurt your tongue to call me "Sire, Polonius".

Hamlet

If it doesn't hurt your ears.

Polonius

Right. You will lodge with the pigs, or under the trees,

because you love the coldness of the evenings. Good night, swineherd. (To Ophelia) I'm going to tell the story to our neighbors and to your fiancée, dear girl. It's worth the trouble—They really going to laugh.

Ophelia

Father —why don't you send him away?

Polonius

(Low) Because, if I had someone else under hand, I would make an example of justice in him. Ah, say that your old dad doesn't do what he can to distract you. Goodbye, my Ophelia.

Ophelia

You are going to drink again.

Polonius

Will you shut up! I leave you your Hamlet. He is quite inoffensive. (Polonius moves away majestic and sneering)

Hamlet

Ophelia. (She starts to retreat) I beg you, Ophelia.

Ophelia

Don't call me Ophelia.

Hamlet

Dame Ophelia.

Ophelia

That seems more fitting to me.

Hamlet

It is.

Ophelia

What have you to say to me?

Hamlet

I see with pleasure that you are well.

Ophelia

(Shrugging her shoulders) Good evening.

Hamlet

You are hard. I knew you more tender. You had a little heart—I said. I see that your little heart was like your charming body—it had a tendency to inflate and swell up.

Ophelia

You are indeed the son of a coachman! You have no vanity. I would have preferred to die than come back.

Hamlet

I came back where you were.

Ophelia

You were thinking of finding your wife.

Hamlet

In my heart for a long time, for a long while you were no longer my wife. I came to see, if by chance, I was not still your husband.

Ophelia

(Offended) Never! Oh, never again!

Hamlet

(Gently) You are right. One must keep one's rank—it's necessary to keep one's rank. When ours is annulled you are going to make a fine marriage?

Ophelia

You will learn in time! You'll see the procession pass. Good night.

Hamlet

(Mournfully) Dame Ophelia, you hold me at a distance, as if for many years already, I'd been sleeping with the pigs I keep.

Ophelia

Don't come near me.

Hamlet

You close your lips and squeeze your nostrils before an unfortunate as if you weren't of noble blood.

Ophelia

It's really something for you to judge—

Hamlet

I'm not judging, I'm not judging, I'm a poor street person, the son of a stable boy who watches the great lords pass and compares their elevation to their rank. It's an amusement of an unemployed worker. I am really unemployed, Dame Ophelia.

Ophelia

You'll be given work.

Hamlet

Yes, I don't detest pigs.

Ophelia

Then join them.

Hamlet

Dame Ophelia, you who possess the joy of satisfied rancor and of satisfied vanity. Won't you do anything to ameliorate my situation?

Ophelia

Don't expect anything from me. You are nothing to me.

Hamlet

Oh, I was speaking of a totally material amelioration. The nights are cool, I'm going to sleep under the trees.

Ophelia

Why not go sleep with the swine? They'll keep you warm.

Hamlet

Because of the stench. I request to accustom myself to it little by little! I had habits.

Ophelia

(Taking from behind the door a crude and dirty blanket) Here! Sleep in this under your tree. It's all I can do for you.

Hamlet

Thanks again, Dame Ophelia.

Ophelia

(Who's had a malicious idea) Perhaps you are hungry?

Hamlet

Like an ordinary man who hasn't eaten.

Ophelia

We have no intention to let you die of hunger—there's some soup for you.

Hamlet

Thanks. I'm going to find it in the kitchen.

Ophelia

(Smiling) No—they'll bring it to you.

Hamlet

Thanks again, Dame Ophelia, you have no rancor.

Ophelia

I pity you. (She leaves, very dignified)

Hamlet

Ah—fattened little serpent. But I have such pity for myself that the pity of others doesn't reach me. (Night comes on. Lights in the windows of Polonius, Phelia opens the door and emerges with a tureen of soup on her hand)

Phelia

Hamlet!

Hamlet

Yes—

Phelia

He's back.

Hamlet

Yes.

Phelia

(Brightened up) Oh—lord Hamlet. Did you come back to seek me? (Hamlet looks at her without comprehending) You are here. You are here. You aren't going to leave again?

Hamlet

Leave again? Oh, no, I've found a position. You are still here. They kept you? Where are you going?

Phelia

To take this tureen of soup to a beggar on behalf of Dame Ophelia.

Hamlet

Let me have it.

Phelia

It's for a beggar.

Hamlet

It's for me.

Phelia

Oh, you are poor?

Hamlet

Yes.

Phelia

So poor?

Hamlet

A beggar—

Phelia

I thought you were heading armies or King of Denmark by now. I was waiting without hope—but I was still waiting.

Hamlet

For what?

Phelia

That one day you would pass by here with your soldiers or that you'd come back, preceded by your heralds from curiosity to see if someone was waiting for you.

Hamlet

Ah!

Phelia

I did right to wait. It's him! It's really him.

Hamlet

A poor beggar.

Phelia

No one knows how he will return. (Clapping her hands) He's come back! He's come back!

Hamlet

Yes to be a swineherd.

Phelia

What pigs?

Hamlet

Those here. Polonius has hired me for this work. It's really to please me. His pigs could be kept by themselves. He's only got two.

Phelia

Three now—

Hamlet

One more—one less.

Phelia

You are no longer a great person.

Hamlet

I never was one—except in a notional sense—and that by error.

Phelia

(Delighted) It's true? Really true?

Hamlet

As true as if Kings knew how to handle horses, they could do without stable boys. It could be a great economy.

Phelia

(Breathing heavily) You are nothing?

Hamlet

A little man.

Phelia

And you will tend pigs here? Forever.

Hamlet

As long as God keeps them in health and in life.

Phelia

Oh—so much the better. Oh—how happy I am.

Hamlet

Ah!

Phelia

I didn't dare to have such a beautiful dream.

Hamlet

Ah!

Phelia

Ah—how less proud your heart is! You are unhappy, really?

Hamlet

A little, yes—

Phelia

Oh—I didn't dare to hope for so much. (Jumping with joy, Hamlet looks at her) Oh! Hamlet! My sweet lord!

Hamlet

Don't call a swineherd, lord!

Phelia

But you are my lord, mine! What was done to you? Where does your heart hurt? Tell me.

Hamlet

No.

Phelia

No! Don't tell me. I'll figure it out. I will console you without knowing. Hamlet, you will give me your hand, your little hand.

Hamlet

Yes—it was refined and white.

Phelia

Oh—see how dark mine are. And yours so fine and fragile.

Hamlet

Why? Yes—I ought to have inherited hands rough and red. Nature deceived itself in the distribution of hands. It also puts hearts in breasts where they have no place. But everything straightens out. All returns to order and there are always pigs to herd for children of stable boys. Brave animals!

Phelia

Hamlet! I don't understand. Tell me.

Hamlet

It's simple and filial. I am going to tend the pigs here in memory of my father who wasn't King and who tended horses.

Phelia

Oh! Hamlet. You are going to be able to live like a farm hand? You have such delicate taste.

Hamlet

I stole them. I'm going to return them. My paternal

blood will assist me. In short what did my father know? Noises of the anvil, the odor of the stable litter, the breath of horses—the taste of bad wine—the skirts of dishwashers—and one day, by chance, the silky bed of a Queen where he ought to have smelled funny. I can indeed accustom myself to the oinking of pigs, to a bed of dung—to soup that's brought to me—and

Phelia

And to me?

Hamlet

Phelia.

Phelia

I'm a dishwasher—look at my skirt.

Hamlet

Phelia you are pretty, you are very clever—that would annoy me.

Phelia

Protect me!

Hamlet

No.

Phelia

Protect me!

Hamlet

You insist on it?

Phelia

Hamlet you must protect me, you didn't come back looking for me—but you must take me—"because I am here!"

Hamlet

If you insist. But, truly you aren't disgusted and you've chosen a bad time. You come to me when I am so ashamed of myself.

Phelia

I also came to you when you were so proud of yourself.

Hamlet

Shut up! Shut up!

Phelia

As for me, Hamlet, I don't see any change. Your outfit is dusty, I'll wash it, and I will comb your tangled hair.

But you haven't changed. You are small lad, Hamlet, and you weren't big.

Hamlet

Ah! In those days, neither—you didn't admire me?

Phelia

I loved you so much and I love you so much. (He lies down. She's seated near him and cradles his head in her lap)

Hamlet

Ophelia, if I left you this night, if I must still do you harm and never love you, you wouldn't want to sleep in the lake near the water lilies?

Phelia

Ah, Hamlet!

Hamlet

You wouldn't do it?

Phelia

No, Hamlet; I would keep living and waiting for you, because I know that you need me.

Hamlet

(Very sad) Yes.

Phelia

You won't leave?

Hamlet

No—not now—why?

Phelia

(Cradling him) Sleep, Hamlet.

Hamlet

I'd like to sleep.

Phelia

Sleep, don't think of anything. We will be just the two of us. When we have a bit of money, we'll buy a field—then another—then some animals—then a house—and then—my Hamlet will see all he'll have. Sleep. Sleep.

Hamlet

Swineherd.

Phelia

Hush! Hush! (Sings) By boat, In my boat—I'll go see—

Hamlet

Oh! No! Not that song! Not now!

Phelia

Why, Hamlet? If the song that cradled you when you were little no longer cradles you—it's because you've become a bad man. No—no—he hasn't gone bad—no—no—

(Sings) By horse, On my horse—(She's on the point of dozing off) Hamlet. I'm a little cold. Let me stay near you. Oh—I'm fine. I'm going to love you for life—sleep, sleep. You see—I'm sleeping—(In her sleep) You won't hurt me now.

Hamlet

No.

Phelia

(Sighing) He mustn't do that to me.

Hamlet

No, Phelia—I won't do that to you I swear it—But

I'm no longer happy about it. (Hamlet closes his eyes. Silence. Polonius appears, swollen with wine and staggering)

Polonius

I swore to Ophelia not to drink anymore. But my will is weak. To abstain, that's the big thing. It's still more difficult to abstain than to have an opinion. On the other hand, when a man's drunk beyond his capacity he ought not to tell stories. Intoxication from one's own wit—inebriates more surely than wine. The day when a man knows how to abstain, to exercise his wit without recourse to it, he will be the equal of God—God on earth. To abstain—that's the secret of high politics. (He takes a few steps and collapses near Hamlet and Phelia)

Heavens Phelia in the arms of a man! Oh! Oh! Clasping a man. Oh! Oh! And head on his breast—against his heart, as they say. Oh! Oh! (Recognizing Hamlet) It's Hamlet—Oh—My swineherd—

Oh! Oh! What a lack of modesty. At my door. Under Ophelia's window. A man for whom I had not enough attention-- so that I took him for someone important.

Their bodies are touching each other in an indecent manner. I don't like indecency. And I've always considered all sexual closeness in which I had no share—indecent. To abstain. (He approaches, very troubled and in a thick voice)

Phelia! Phelia! You have beautiful hair, my pretty. What I see of your leg looks seductive to me and promising of intimate satisfaction. Phelia leave your swineherd, my pigeon—Come to the room above the kitchen. Your leg please me, Phelia, I assure you. I am capable of showing you that I appreciate a pretty leg.— Phelia, you are sleeping, my young kitty-cat (Goes to her knees, hand hesitating over Phelia's leg)

I swore to my virtuous companion on her death bed— not to touch a woman again—in a word, to abstain. Dear companion I kept this oath.—Oh—that leg— oh—oh!

I kept it from fidelity and because was made with less impetuous with age—and besides it manifests the grandeur of God. Phelia—I feel that I cannot resist— on account of this beautiful leg—

Phelia my beautiful nightingale, you must come above the kitchen. (Shakes her gently)

Phelia!—Listen, listen to me.

Phelia

(Awaking abruptly) What?

Polonius

It's me.

Phelia

What do you want?

Polonius

Come with me to the room above the kitchen.

Phelia

(Frightened) To do what?

Polonius

She asks! Innocent and clever!—My poor wife was like that. But she didn't have your legs. Pussy! What a pussy! (Phelia gestures) Yes! Let me see your legs.

Phelia

Get out.

Polonius

My pussy.

Phelia

Get out!

Polonius

My pussy! I am a tomcat in full strength. Listen.

Phelia

Enough! Enough!

Polonius

(Raising his voice) Phelia!

Phelia

Ah, shut up. You'll wake him.

Polonius

(Lowering his voice) You are right. We don't need him. You think of everything my pussy. Come, let's leave him to his pigs—and his dreams of grandeur. I'm sure he's counting pigs in his dreams.

Phelia

Get out! Don't touch me!

Polonius

Come! The two of us are going to dream. We'll dream awake, you know! I am a happy cat, you know. Without seeming to be—you know. (Hamlet moves)

Phelia

(In despair) oh—he's going to wake up. Let him sleep—He's so unhappy.

Polonius

Yes, he is. You are right. You've got a kind heart. You are devoting yourself to consoling him. That's nice. It's a veritable ecstasy of charity. Be charitable for me, too, Phelia. I'm an old tom cat dying without his pussy. (She gets up and moves away, terrified, he follows her)

Have pity on my need of virile expansion. Come into the room, you want to, you want to! Above the kitchen. (He holds her in his arms) God will know your taste. You will have been charitable twice in one night. What a beautiful night for you my clever darling. You will be a saint of charity, I tell you. (She runs off, uttering a little scream; Hamlet opens his eyes, listening)

Phelia

Get out of here or I'll run away.

Polonius

I will follow you, my squirrel.

Phelia

I'll drown myself if you touch me.

Polonius

You'll get your legs wet.

Phelia

Release me!

Polonius

I will give you a dress, an old dress of my daughter's.

Phelia

(In tears, taking low) Leave me alone! Leave me alone!

Polonius

The silver comb of my sainted wife who is near God! What do you say to that, huh? Huh? Come against me. You'll die of envy. (He pulls her strongly against himself. She scratches his face) Oh, naughty. Yes, scratch me, go ahead—those are pussy games! Come or I will kick Hamlet out tomorrow.

Phelia

I will follow him. I love him and I don't want to see you anymore.

Polonius

(Leans over her, crushing her wrist) Come, or I'll kick him out immediately with blows of a stick.

Phelia

No—Let him sleep tonight.

Polonius

Then come or I'll wake him.

Phelia

No.

Polonius

I'll toss a bucket of water on him. It will spread over his skin through the holes in his clothes.

Phelia

I beg you. (She cries)

Polonius

Come show me your legs.

Phelia

Oh!

Polonius

I'm going to get the bucket.

Phelia

(Crying, ready to follow Polonius) Oh, Hamlet.

Polonius

The bucket?

Phelia

No.

Polonius

Then, come! (He pulls her, consenting she takes a step to follow him)

Hamlet

(Motionless, eyes open) Polonius is a swine!

Phelia

(A cry) Hamlet.

Polonius

It's nothing. He's dreaming.

Hamlet

A swine—a mere swine.

Phelia

(Stretching towards him, choked voice) Hamlet—

Polonius

Don't go wake him! He fidgets.

Hamlet

So I'm a character that they fear to wake up.

Polonius

(Speechless) Huh?

Phelia

Hamlet! My Hamlet! I wanted to let you sleep. (She's in his arms)

Polonius

(Trying to get hold of himself) We wanted to let you sleep.

Hamlet

(Striding slowly toward him) Ah.

Polonius

(Intimidated and deferential) Yes—you were sleeping good, Hamlet—like a child dreaming—

Hamlet

Who was dreaming.

Polonius

You were talking in your dreams.

Hamlet

What was I saying?

Polonius

Words—Lord Hamlet—If I said, Lord—

Hamlet

Polonius—you are a swine.

Polonius

Yes—that's what you said—

Hamlet

Polonius, get out.

Polonius

(Pointing to Ophelia) I was explaining to her that it is cold here at night.—I was advising her to go to the room above the kitchen—if you care to go there, too.

Hamlet

I am therefore a great personage that I see you so cowardly before me.

Polonius

I consider—

Hamlet

Polonius, get out. I'm kicking you out.

Polonius

What's he say?

Hamlet

Get out! And before you go, beg my pardon—

Polonius

Hamlet, I am indulgent. I pardon your youth, but it's impossible for me—

Hamlet

(A little pale, but unmoved) Polonius, ask pardon of your swineherd.

Polonius

(stammering) Hamlet, dear Hamlet.

Hamlet

As if he were your Lord.

Polonius

He's mad! Hamlet, be reasonable!

Hamlet

On your knees, Polonius, face to the ground—before her and me!

Polonius

Hamlet, I'm going to call!

Hamlet

On your knees!

Polonius

Hamlet, I regret not having been able to abstain. But,

on my knees, I cannot.

Hamlet

On your knees.

Polonius

A bastard—a son of a stable boy!

Hamlet

(Recoiling) Yes—yes—he's right—I am nothing.

Phelia

Oh my sweet Lord. You are everything to me!

Hamlet

(Eyes bright) It's true. She consented to drown herself or weep with disgust on the bed of an old geezer, rather than disturb my sleep.

Phelia

(Forcefully) Yes—yes—yes.

Hamlet

I am a man to die for. (He leaps on Polonius and throws him to his knees)

Polonius

(Overwhelmed) Help, help!

Hamlet

(Abruptly Hamlet strangles Polonius. A pause. Polonius falls) Like a bad beast. (A pause) This drunk disgusted me. There are thus disgusts more powerful than disgust with oneself. I am still of a base condition. Phelia, do you think—tell me, that a child of a stable boy can resent such disgusts?

Phelia

Oh, no.

Hamlet

No, is it? What would a servant have done in my place when he wanted to drag you away. (Points to the body)

Phelia

He would have let him do it; he would have feared for his wages.

Hamlet

Wouldn't he?

Phelia

Yes, he'd have pretended not to wake up.

Hamlet

Right?

Phelia

After that perhaps he'd have wept.

Hamlet

Wretches of base birth weep when wrong is done them, right?

Phelia

Surely.

Hamlet

I didn't weep. I wasn't capable of weeping.

Phelia

No, no—you never cry.

Hamlet

But perhaps there are valets who do not weep, and whose heart accumulates a resentment, a rage which would do injury to others, and those who wronged them.

Phelia

Yes, Lord, I've known some; they are like that.

Hamlet

I have neither rage nor bitterness. I am calm, Phelia—and almost completely happy. (At Polonius scream lights were lit in the house. Through the branches torches circulate. Ophelia appears)

Ophelia

There was a scream. Where is my father?

Hamlet

He's there, Madame—He's dead.

Ophelia

(With a great scream) Ah! Help! Help!

Hamlet

I killed him, Madame, for the second time, and without anger; quite naturally like a man who exercises the right of life and death. (To Phelia) Do you think, Phelia, that a man of the people would confess his crime with so much serenity?

Phelia

He would tremble, Lord—He would hide his face in his hands. He couldn't smile the way you are smiling.

Hamlet

Yes—isn't that right? You see me, Phelia: hands at my sides, lips at ease, heart calm. (To Ophelia, pointing to Polonius) Madame, from drunkenness he got killed. He was a cowardly swine who played in the great world—Peace to this body which had no soul!

Ophelia

Don't come near me. Help! Captain! Captain!

Hamlet

You're right to call, we must transport the remains. I will salute it as it passes. (To Phelia) Right? Phelia. What delicacy. Are these the manners of a swineherd or those of a great Lord?

Phelia

Of a great Lord, Lord Hamlet.

Hamlet

Aren't they. I feel so indeed. That's the way I am.

Phelia

Yes, that's the way you are.

Hamlet

And since childhood!

Phelia

(Throwing herself at his feet and hugging his knees) My dear Lord.

Hamlet

Phelia, you truly understand me, you are the only one who knows me.

Phelia

I love you—

Hamlet

But—I intimidate you a little, don't I?

Phelia

Yes—

Hamlet

You admire me—

Phelia

Oh, yes—

Hamlet

In that case, I love you, too. (He offers her his hand and pulls her up—neighbors including Waldemar, Hans and others enter with torches, armed with sticks and pikes, the Captain, helmet on his head holds his armor in one hand, sword in the other)

(Noise and consternation around the body of Polonius, tearful explanations from Ophelia, then the Captain—threatening, huge, goes toward Hamlet)

Captain

It's you who killed him?

Ophelia

And she urged him to do it.

Captain

It's you who killed him? (A threatening circle surrounds the young people)

Hamlet

Yes. I killed him. Ah, gentlemen! It is suitable to give this poor man a funeral worthy of his past grandeur. He was chamberlain of the King, my father. Decent funeral, right, gentlemen? What? What's wrong? Why are you looking at me with round eyes like open pits? What have I said that's astonishing? Go, withdraw! I need to rest tonight. Tomorrow I will give orders.— Come, Phelia. (A burst of sonorous and nasty laughter "Imbecile!". Listen to him "In the river") And why are you making a circle around me? Don't you know me, I am Hamlet, Prince of Denmark!

(Nervous laughter "Look at him!" "Dangerous mad man!" " We know his story.")

Captain

I knew your father, you know. He often groomed my horse. He ended up hanged—the son won't finish any better.

Hamlet

(Recoiling a little) Phelia!

Phelia

Yes.

Hamlet

They hurl this story at my head. They are mistaken, aren't they? They are workers in revolt?

Phelia

Yes, Lord, see their eyes! I see yours.

Hamlet

(Reassured, very loud) Go home! Conserve yourselves for your workman's scandals.

Voices

You're going to die. In the water, swineherd. A good blow of the saber behind the head.

Hamlet

(To the Captain) Make them go home, after which you will stand guard before our door. (The Captain, hands on hips laughs loudly—strides toward Hamlet and knocks him over with a backhand—sending him rolling in the dust)

Captain

Just the two of us.

Ophelia

(From a distance) Kill him!

Phelia

(Screaming) Hamlet!

Ophelia

Her too! Both of them. (The Captain pulls his sword and strides toward Hamlet)

Hans

(To Captain) Something much more amusing! Stone them to death. Let's all stand right here. Three stones each, and each in his turn.

Waldemar

Now there's an idea. Who'll throw the first stone? (They draw a line in the ground, pick up stones, arguing. Hamlet and Ophelia remain alone)

Phelia

You are sick.

Hamlet

I didn't defend myself. A man of the people would have

tried. You observed that?

Phelia

I'm afraid, Hamlet.

Hamlet

Afraid?

Phelia

Yes.

Hamlet

Why? You see—They've distanced themselves. They understood, they're standing at a deferential distance. (To crowd) Go, my good friends. I pardon you, Captain. Don't be afraid, Ophelia. You are trembling like a butterfly at the end of fingers—take away the body of the unfortunate Polonius. I pardon him, too. (A first stone, then a second)

Phelia

Lord Hamlet.

Hamlet

Stones.

Phelia

We are going to die.

Hamlet

They are many to throw stones?

Phelia

(Hanging on him) They are going to kill us.

Hamlet

You think so? (Suddenly brightening up) Yes, but from a distance. They have laid down a line, you see, between them and me. They don't dare cross it!

Phelia

Hamlet, it would have been so good to live!

Hamlet

Yes—possibly—They are afraid! They are afraid! They are afraid! Do you think that a swineherd could intimidate clodhoppers?

Phelia

(Weakly) No.

Hamlet

Speak up!

Phelia

No.

Hamlet

(Triumphant) Ah!

Phelia

Hamlet, I didn't want to die.

Hamlet

Save yourself! Live without me.

Phelia

(A scream) Oh, no!

Hamlet

No? You accept to die here?

Phelia

Yes—

Hamlet

Gladly?

Phelia

Yes.

Hamlet

Tell me, Ophelia. (She staggers and falls, he rushes to her) Oh, wait! Answer. Don't die yet. Oh! I am wounded! A word! Phelia—Oh they hit hard! If you die without answering me, there's no use in your dying. Do you hear me? Open your eyes. Think about me again, Phelia!

Phelia

Yes—

Hamlet

The one who accepts the death of others in his honor—the most dear death—speak up, little love, who still is thinking only of herself—he has a well-born soul, right? Who is he?

Phelia

(With effort) Lord Hamlet—

Hamlet

A Lord. You said it! Yes! Yes! Yes! (Another stone, he falls to his knees) Answer again—Who is he who all pursued furiously?

Phelia

A great man.

Hamlet

What is he who remains alone?—

Phelia

The greatest!

Hamlet

The first. Speak up!

Phelia

Yes, Lord.

Hamlet

(Exalted, stands up) Ah—I knew it! The Reverend

was deceived. Sleep, Phelia. (To others) Good night, gentlemen—you are my vassals. (A final stone. He falls. More stones. Then the Captain drags Ophelia away, carrying the body of Polonius)

Voices

There they are dead! What to do with them? Tomorrow put them in a sack. They'll go to the bottom of the lake. That's good enough for a dishwasher and a swineherd!

(They vanish—dying, Phelia rises and leans over him singing)

Phelia

By boat, In my boat—

Hamlet

(Also rising) What?

Phelia

Lord Hamlet.

Hamlet

Good night.

Phelia

Good night. (They make an effort and get to their knees)

Hamlet

Gentlemen—Barons of the Realm, Archbishops, Constable, I present to you, Phelia, your Queen.

Phelia

Yes, Hamlet—I love you.

Hamlet

Our wife, who loves us. Gentlemen—we must drive away this evil stable boy.

Phelia

My King!

Hamlet

Yes. (They both collapse)

CURTAIN

ABOUT FRANK J. MORLOCK

Frank J. Morlock has written and translated many plays since retiring from the legal profession in 1992. His translations have also appeared on Project Gutenberg, the Alexandre Dumas Père web page, Literature in the Age of Napoléon, Infinite Artistries.com, and Munsey's (formerly Blackmask). In 2006 he received an award from the North American Jules Verne Society for his translations of Verne's plays. He lives and works in México.

www.ingramcontent.com/pod-product-compliance
Lightning Source LLC
LaVergne TN
LVHW041617070426
835507LV00008B/286